Dahae Lee
Public Space in Transition

Urban Studies

Dahae Lee works as a research associate at the Faculty of Spatial Planning from the Technical University of Dortmund (TU Dortmund). Prior to her PhD at the TU Dortmund, she studied geography and urban planning at Humboldt University of Berlin and University College London. Her research focuses on public space governance and urban transformation.

Dahae Lee

Public Space in Transition

Co-production and Co-management of Privately Owned Public Space in Seoul and Berlin

[transcript]

PhD thesis submitted to the Faculty of Spatial Planning at the Technical University of Dortmund

Date of Defence: November 30, 2021

Bibliographic information published by the Deutsche Nationalbibliothek
The Deutsche Nationalbibliothek lists this publication in the Deutsche National-bibliografie; detailed bibliographic data are available in the Internet at http://dnb.d-nb.de

First published in 2022 by transcript Verlag, Bielefeld
© Dahae Lee

Cover layout: Kordula Röckenhaus, Bielefeld

Print-ISBN 978-3-8376-6232-0
PDF-ISBN 978-3-8394-6232-4
https://doi.org/10.14361/9783839462324
ISSN of series: 2747-3619
eISSN of series: 2747-3635

Contents

Acknowledgements

This book is a result of my Ph.D. research. Throughout the writing of this book, I have received a great deal of support and assistance. I want to take a moment to thank them.

First and foremost, I would like to thank my supervisor, Professor Dr. Karsten Zimmermann, who guided me throughout the whole process. Your guidance helped me to choose the right direction and successfully complete my Ph.D. I appreciate your continuous support and all the opportunities I was given to further my research.

I am also extremely grateful to my supervisor, Professor Dr. Angela Million. Your insightful feedback pushed me to sharpen my thinking and brought my work to a higher level.

Gratitude also goes to my colleague, Dr. Patricia Feiertag, for reviewing part of the book and giving valuable comments. Sunnam Won and James Hogg also deserve thanks for the final polish.

I would also like to acknowledge all the interviewees who provided useful information for the research.

Finally, I could not have completed this book without the support of my family who provided stimulating discussions as well as happy distractions to rest my mind outside my research.

Abstract

Public spaces are not solely the products of planners and architects; they are produced by and within a society. As society keeps changing, so too does public space. Economic, socio-cultural and political dynamics have resulted in the emergence of three characteristics of contemporary public space: high-quality public space, diverse and secured public space, and co-produced public space. However, less research has been conducted on the characteristics of public space in a transitional context, whereby societal changes are far more dynamic in terms of pace and intensity. Thus, this research aims to investigate public space in a transitional context, specifically in relation to its provision and management. Teheran-ro in Seoul and the Mediaspree area in Berlin were selected for an empirical study as they have a history of rapid change. Teheran-ro underwent a process of rapid development after the Korean War, while the Mediaspree area also experienced radical change due to a programme of property investment after the fall of socialism and the subsequent German reunification. Multiple sources of data and research methods (i.e., comparative analysis, document analysis, expert interview and site visit and analysis) are used.

The findings suggest that even though the drivers of transformation in Teheran-ro and Mediaspree area are different, common challenges arise, especially the public sector's lack of capability to provide and manage public space alone. In response, in both cases, the public sector has engaged private sector entities – in the form of privately owned public space/s (POPS) – to share costs, rights and responsibilities regarding public space provision and management. Planning instruments used for the provision and management of POPS in both cases are identified and analysed. In addition, a number of POPS in Teheran-ro and Mediaspree area were visited, analysed and evaluated to better understand these planning instruments as well as their outcomes. The results are compared to identify the uniqueness of planning instruments in each case as well as their strengths and weaknesses. Based on the results, the research makes a number of policy recommendations for cities undergoing radical change and facing high development pressure, which are therefore seeking effective ways to engage other stakeholders in public space provision and management.

List of Figures and Tables

Figures

Tables

List of Abbreviations

AEG: Anschutz Entertainment Group
AGBauGB: Gesetz zur Ausführung des Baugesetzbuchs
BauGB: Baugesetzbuch
BauO Bln: Bauordnung für Berlin
Bezirksamt FHKR: Bezirksamt Friedrichshain-Kreuzberg von Berlin
BEP: Bereichsentwicklungsplanung
BGB: Bürgerliches Gesetzbuch
BNatSchG: Bundesnaturschutzgesetz
B-Plan: Bebauungsplan
BverfGE: Bundesverfassungsgericht
DUP: District Unit Plan(ning)
FNP: Flächennutzungsplan
LaPro: Landschaftsprogramm
SenStadt: Senatsverwaltung für Stadtentwicklung
SenSW: Senatsverwaltung für Stadtentwicklung und Wohnen
SenUVK: Senatsverwaltung für Umwelt, Verkehr und Klimaschutz
WEP: Wasserlagenentwicklungsplan

Chapter 1. Introduction

1.1.   Research objective, questions and methodology

Public spaces have been popular research topics. The large amount of international literature on public space suggests that there is a lot of knowledge on the subject; yet, there are areas that are relatively underexplored (Van Melik, 2008). The characteristics of public space in a transitional context is one such area. The lack of knowledge is regrettable as events that trigger the transformation of cities can occur anywhere, anytime and in any form. This research aims to investigate public space in a transitional context, specifically in relation to its provision and management, and in response to the following four research questions:

- What challenges does the public sector face in providing and managing public space in a transitional context?
- How does the public sector address these challenges?
- What do the outcomes of the respective planning instruments look like in reality?
- What implications does the research provide for cities undergoing rapid transformation and facing high development pressure, and which are looking for ways to engage other stakeholders, including the private sector, in public space provision and management?

Two sites in transitional contexts were selected: Teheran-ro in Seoul and Mediaspree area in Berlin. At first glance, the two areas seem to have nothing in common, but they share experiences of radical transformation. Teheran-ro underwent a process of rapid urbanisation after the Korean War, while Mediaspree area also experienced radical change due to a programme of property investment after the fall of socialism and the subsequent German reunification.

To answer the research questions, multiple sources of data and research methods (comparative analysis, document analysis, expert interview and site visit and analysis) have been used. Through such triangulation, this prevents the 'accusation that a study's findings are simply an artefact of a single method, a single source, or a single investigator's bias' (Patton, 1990, 470).

1.2.   Significance of the research

The research makes three contributions. First, by researching public space in a transitional context, this book intends to inform urban planners and policymakers about the challenges they may face in terms of providing and managing public space in rapidly changing situations. Moreover, the research increases the knowledge of urban planners and policymakers about planning instruments relevant to privately owned public space/s (hereafter POPS). It is important to broaden such knowledge since POPS are, after all, produced and managed within the regulatory environment; as a result, their quality and use are directly affected by the instruments deployed. Policy recommendations drawn from the research results aim to improve planning practice. In addition to practical contributions, this research also adds to the body of knowledge on POPS in Germany. Although POPS are nothing new in the country, research on this topic has been largely lacking. Research on POPS is crucial since they are contested spaces; insufficient knowledge can negatively affect the members of the public who use them.

It is important to mention here that the aim is not to advocate POPS. My argument is, rather, that if private involvement in providing and managing public space is inevitable, as the cases in this book illustrate, it should take place in a proper manner. Increasing knowledge within the public sector about planning instruments relevant to POPS is crucial so that it can maximise the benefits and minimise the negative consequences of POPS.

1.3.   Outline of the book

This book is divided into eight chapters (see Table 1.1). After the introduction, the international literature on the topic is reviewed in Chapter 2. The research methodology is described in Chapter 3. Chapter 4 attempts to answer the first research question by examining the challenges that the transformations of Teheran-ro and Mediaspree area brought about in relation to public space. Chapters 5 and 6 then present the findings in response to the second research question by analysing the specific planning instruments used for the provision and management of POPS in both cases. Chapter 7 investigates the outcomes of these planning instruments. Conclusions are drawn in the final chapter along with key policy recommendations.

Table 1.1 Outline of the book

Part 1: Introducing research topic	Introduction (Chapter 1)
	Literature review (Chapter 2)
	Methodology (Chapter 3)
Part 2: Exploring the provision and management of public space in a transitional context	Challenges of providing and managing public space in a transitional context (Chapter 4)
	Planning instruments relevant to POPS (Chapters 5 and 6)
	Outcomes of planning instruments (Chapter 7)
Part 3: Summarising the research results	Conclusions with policy recommendations (Chapter 8)

Source: Author's own table.

Chapter 2. Public space in transition

This chapter includes a review of the international literature on public space, and it is divided into five sections. First, the definition and dimensions of public space are reviewed to introduce the research topic and determine the boundaries of the research. In the second section, the changing nature of public space is described through an analysis of the effects of societal shifts (e.g., economic, sociocultural and political) on public space. The next section specifically examines the concepts of co-production of public space and POPS, which is a type of co-produced public space. Following an overview of the research topic, additional information is provided regarding the context of rapid urbanisation and post-socialism. A research gap is identified at the end of the literature review, and it is described in the final section.

2.1. Public space – definition and dimensions

The term "public space" has multiple definitions because it has been studied within a variety of disciplines (Neugebauer & Rekhviashvili, 2015). The broad meaning and varied conceptualisation of the term may cause confusion. The fact that different authors have used different terms (e.g., urban public space, public space, public place, public realm, public sphere) without offering a clear definition or interpretation further complicates the situation. Many authors have been vague in their use of these terms in relation to one another (Varna, 2014). It is a daunting task to define public space; however, an attempt must be made to determine the boundary of the present research. A review of the literature indicates that there are a number of key dimensions used to define public space, including ownership, management, accessibility, and inclusiveness. These four dimensions will be discussed in depth in the following paragraphs.

Ownership, which defines the legal status of a space, is the most straight-forward dimension by which to define public space (Langstraat & Van Melik, 2013). According to De Magalhães (2010), this dimension does not 'necessarily refer to public ownership, but to the rules and mechanisms through which a variety of stakes in a particular public space are recognised in its governance, and through which conflicts and disputes between different stakes can be solved' (563). Indeed, the fact that a space is publicly owned does not guarantee that it possesses the essential qualities of a public space (De Magalhães, 2010). Some public spaces are provided and maintained through state ownership, but private ownership is also possible. In fact, public life increasingly occurs in privately owned settings including cafés, bookstores, bars, and other small private locations (Oldenburg, 1989). Similarly, Worpole and Knox (2007) have argued that 'gathering at the school gate, activities in community facilities, shopping malls, cafés and car boot sales are all arenas where people meet and create places of exchange' (4).

Ownership, in many cases, is directly related to operation in that publicly owned spaces are publicly operated and privately owned spaces are privately operated (Németh & Schmidt, 2011). However, there are also spaces in which ownership and operation are mixed. Hence, four combinations are possible regarding ownership and operation of spaces: (a) publicly owned and operated; (b) publicly owned and privately operated; (c) privately owned and publicly operated; and (d) privately owned and operated (Németh & Schmidt, 2011). In recent years, spaces characterised by mixed ownership and operation have become increasingly popular (Katz, 2006).

Maintenance, another important dimension of public space, can be divided into three categories, i.e., cleanliness, provision of amenities and the practice of control (Lee & Scholten, 2022). The maintenance of a space refers to the manner in which a space is cared for on a daily basis and the provision of amenities in the space (Langstraat & Van Melik, 2013). A well-lit, clean, and inviting public space in which amenities for basic needs are provided encourages access and use, whereas a lack of amenities and over- or under-management may discourage access to and use of the space (Varna & Tiesdell, 2010). Maintenance can also refer to the practice of control in a space (Langstraat & Van Melik, 2013) through overt techniques (e.g., the presence of surveillance cameras and security guard) and more subtle cues and codes (Whyte, 1988). However, the presence of control does not reduce the publicness of public space; rather, the determining factor is the purpose of control (Varna & Tiesdell, 2010). For example, the posting of a set of rules does not affect publicness negatively if the aim of the rules is to exclude anti-social be-haviours. However, the setting of rules in a public space becomes problematic if the aim is to protect the interests of the powerful.

Accessibility is another significant dimension of public space, as ev-idenced by several definitions in the literature. For example, the Dutch Ministry of Housing, Spatial Planning and the Environment (VROM, 2001, as cited in Van Melik, 2008) offers a notably broad and inclusive definition of public space as 'all freely accessible spaces' (2). Similarly, Orum and Neal (2009) define public space as 'all areas that are open and accessible to all members of the public in a society in principle, though not necessarily in practice' (2). Carr et al. (1992) also emphasises accessibility by stating that public spaces 'are usually open and accessible to the public' (50). Accessibility includes whether members of the public can reach and enter the space, as well as the amount of effort required to do so (Varna & Tiesdell, 2010). Public spaces that are well located within a city's movement pattern are likely to attract people (Hillier, 1996). The design of public space is another important part of accessibility. Entrances or thresholds are seen as a barrier; thus, public spaces that do not have such physical entrances have greater potential for use (Langstraat & Van Melik, 2013). Visual accessibility is also a crucial factor in that public spaces can only be used if they are visible from the outside (Lee & Scholten, 2022).

The final dimension of public space is inclusiveness, which refers to the degree to which 'a place meets the demands of different individuals and groups' (Langstraat & Van Melik, 2013, 435). Public spaces that are designed for and used by different types of users are considered inclusive (Langstraat & Van Melik, 2013). As Franck and Paxson (1989) assert, 'the greater diversity of people and activities allowed and manifested in a space, the greater its publicness' (131). The core elements of inclusiveness include the specific phys-ical configuration and design elements that support use of and activity in a public space. Inclusive public spaces accommodate users' needs for comfort, relaxation, passive and active engagement, discovery, and display (Carr et al., 1992; Carmona et al., 2010). Public spaces must allow for spontaneity and unscripted, unprogrammed activities in order to encourage engagement, play, and discovery (Stevens, 2007). The notion of "loose space" (i.e., adapt-able, unrestricted, and multifunctional that are both ad hoc and planned; see Frank & Stevens, 2006) is well suited to inclusiveness. Interestingly, public space that 'might appear more public to some might feel less public to others' (Németh & Schmidt, 2011, 12).

In summary, there is no one-size-fits-all definition of public space. Therefore, public space should be considered a multi-dimensional concept with a range of possible dimensions. There are four different models of measuring the publicness of public space that take a multi-dimensional approach:

- Cobweb model by Van Melik, Van Aalst and Van Weesep (2007)
- Tri-axial model by Németh and Schmidt (2011)
- Star model by Varna and Tiesdell (2010)
- OMAI model by Langstraat and Van Melik (2013)

Each of these models is based on a multifaceted definition of public space. Failure to meet the requirements of a single dimension does not necessarily categorise a space as private (Kohn, 2004). These models are useful because they enable measurements of the publicness of public space, which in turn allows comparisons of the publicness of different public spaces.

2.2.   The changing nature of public space

Public spaces are produced by and within a society, as sociologist Henri Lefebvre (1990) has claimed. As society changes, so does public space. Public space has undergone a number of transitions over time and will continue to evolve in the future. Societal shifts can be classified as economic, sociocultural, and political (Asbeek Brusse et al., 2002, as cited in Van Melik, 2008) and each of these shift types has specific effects on public space. In this section, these dynamics and their effects on public space will be described.

Global economic changes have led to increased investment in public spaces because such investments have proven to be economically lucrative (Van Melik, 2008). Cities compete nationally and internationally so that they can accommodate investments, businesses, tourists, and high-income residents (Madanipour, 2003; Gospodini, 2006; Groth & Corijn, 2005; Short & Kim, 1999), and impressive buildings and events alone are not sufficient (Van Melik, 2008). The presence of public spaces that connect buildings and activities is an important factor for people and companies seeking a new location (Madanipour, 2003). Hence, cities invest in public spaces to make themselves look safe and appealing while also providing a variety of amenities and facilities expected by citizens (Madanipour, 2003). Businesses have also reaped economic benefits from the creation of public spaces (Punter, 1990).

Safe and entertaining public spaces attract people to an area and generate increased economic activity as people spend money in cafés and bars (Van Melik, 2008). Developers often seek to include public space within schematics for new properties while retaining their ownership and maintenance responsibility.

Sociocultural dynamics are closely linked to the trends of individualisation and multiculturalism, both of which have contributed to an increase in the differentiation of urban lifestyles (Florida, 2002). Accordingly, desires and demands related to public space have become differentiated, meaning it is difficult to design neutral public spaces (Van Melik, 2008). In today's heterogeneous society, individual users of public spaces have diverse and competing interests, which may lead to conflicts (Carr et al., 1992; Lofland, 1998; Zukin, 1998). According to Goss (1996), one should not 'blame festival marketplaces for failing to provide equal access to all members of a mystical general public – which does not and cannot exist in an ethnically and class-divided society' (231). To cater to the different needs of the public, therefore, diverse public spaces (e.g., vibrant and commercial, serious and civic, peaceful and relaxing) are created to serve the different needs of the public (Carmona, 2019).

Additionally, members of the public have become increasingly concerned with safety. As Ellin (2001) has argued, 'we no longer go out to mingle with the anonymous urban crowd in the hope of some new unexpected experience or encounter, a characteristic feature of earlier urban life' (875). Although crime is concentrated in specific locations, fear and insecurity are widespread (Brunt, 1996, as cited in Van Melik, 2008). Developers have addressed security concerns by providing enhanced security measures in public spaces. In addition to direct security measures (e.g., supervision by security guards and installation of surveillance cameras), several indirect measures (e.g., hide-approach and the installation of sadistic street furniture) are in use (Van Melik, 2008). Secured public spaces have been developed as people go to controlled areas such as shopping malls, sport arenas, and theme parks.

The trend of increased security has highlighted concerns regarding the privatisation of public spaces. Indeed, scholars such as Michael Sorkin (1992) and Nan Ellin (1999) warned the privatisation of urban space and the subsequent loss of public space in the United States and other parts of the Western world. As Loukaitou-Sideris (1993) described, '[...] privatization is not simply a change of delivery system of a public amenity; it is a process in which the meaning and purposes of public open space are redefined and reshaped in the context of changing socio-economic and political relationships' (160). The key issue of privatisation is that individual private landlords who own and manage private-public spaces can restrict access and control activities in those spaces (Minton, 2006). This issue is controversial issue, and some scholars have argued that the fact that a space is private rather than public 'does not determine either its quality as a place, or its potential role as part of the public realm' (Carmona, 2010, 161).

Finally, political dynamics include democratisation, decentralisation, and the rearrangement of the public and private spheres. Democratisation is achieved by involving the public in decision-making processes regarding public space. By doing so, the government may gain public support for policies and financial cooperation such as tax payments (Van Melik, 2008). Decentralisation and rearrangement of public and private spheres are connected. Due to a lack of available state money, the nation-state often shifts the responsibility for public spaces to local authorities. However, local governments alone are unable and unwilling to bear sole responsibility for public space, due to limited financial resources for investing in public spaces (De Magalhães, 2010; Langstraat & Van Melik, 2013). Thus, local authorities increasingly cooperate with non-municipal actors such as private companies to develop public spaces (Loukaitou-Sideris & Banerjee, 1998; Zukin, 1998; Banerjee, 2001; Carmona et al., 2010). This approach saves government expenses and contributes to the creation of more spectacular and well-maintained spaces.

Scrutiny of the existing research reveals that economic, sociocultural, and political dynamics have important effects on public space. Economic dynamics have increased the quality of public spaces, whereas sociocultural dynamics have led to public spaces that are diverse and secure. Political dynamics have resulted in co-produced public spaces that rely on the engagement of various actors. In summary, contemporary public space constantly evolves to adjust to societal changes, and new forms of public space lead to critical debates.

2.3.   Co-production of public space and POPS

Changes in the use and production of public space reflect wider societal changes. In the previous section, three characteristics of contemporary public space that reflect changes in society were discussed (i.e., high quality, diversity and security, and co-production). This section further examines the concept of co-production of public space and describes POPS, which is a specific type of co-produced public space.

Public space is often regarded as traditional public good (Van Melik & Van der Krabben, 2016). The public sector, particularly local government, is thought to be the party responsible for public space provision and management. However, local governments increasingly lack the budget, incentive, and capacity for public space provision and management, particularly in densely populated cities where public space congests and degrades at a fast pace (Webster, 2007). One solution to preserve the quality of public space is to actively involve private actors (Berding et al., 2010). A wide range of stakeholders have been brought into public space provision and management. These entities share the costs, rights, and responsibilities of public space with the local government (Van Melik & Van der Krabben, 2016). Co-production differs from privatisation in that it implies cooperation rather than a complete transfer of responsibility to the private sector (Stolk, 2013, as citied in Van Melik & Van der Krabben, 2016).

The boundary between public and private spheres regarding public space has become increasingly blurred as a wide array of organisations and people have become involved in the provision and management of public spaces. Many examples of co-produced public spaces exist, particularly in liberal welfare states such as the United States and the United Kingdom. Public-private partnerships for the project organisation, financing, and ownership of public spaces have become increasingly common (Carmona et al., 2019). As a result, various kinds of public spaces have newly emerged. The concept of hybrid space has evolved to encompass the different types of public, semi-public, semi-private, and private spaces (Nisse, 2008). Some examples include business improvement districts, POPS, and conservancies. The remainder of this section will examine the concept and function of POPS.

POPS are 'a mechanism to increase provision of public space, particularly in densely built-up urban areas' (Lee, 2020, 1). These spaces are also referred to as "bonus plazas", because builders receive additional floor-area ratio in exchange for providing and maintaining publicly accessible spaces at the street level (Smithsimon, 2008). The provision of POPS in New York City in 1960s was the first instance where the public goal (i.e., delivery of public space) was met by private builders in order to achieve planning and zoning goals (Smithsimon, 2008; Kayden et al., 2000; Whyte, 1988). The idea of POPS has become increasingly popular and has since been implemented across the United States and around the world (Kayden et al., 2000; Whyte,

1988). Banerjee (2001) has described three key trends that contribute to the rise of POPS: (a) increased use of the market to provide public goods and services; (b) growth of transnational corporate power and prioritisation of the global economy over local public interests; and (c) technologically advanced forms of communication that have altered the character of social relations and redefined traditional conceptions of place and location.

By definition, POPS are hybrid spaces. The government defines the public right to the space and sets rules about the use of the space, whereas the market invests money and is in charge of providing and maintaining the space. The degree of citizens' involvement in POPS varies considerably in different cities and countries. In New York City, for example, non-profit organisations such as Advocates for Privately Owned Public Space and The Municipal Art Society of New York have collaborated to revitalise new and existing POPS by bringing together various actors such as residents and civic artists (APOPS et al., n.d.).

POPS are 'no different than public space in the sense that they are publicly accessible and useable' (Lee, 2020, 3). Although privately owned and managed, POPS must be open to the public as per agreement with the local government, and they are required to meet common standards for public spaces. POPS have several functions that benefit citizens, as summarised by Kang et al. (2009). First of all, the original function of POPS is to provide walking space and resting area. Since POPS are scattered across cities, they can benefit residents by offering a place to rest and interact with others. Secondly, from an ecological perspective, POPS conserve natural resources and improve the environment. Additionally, POPS function from an architectural perspective as outdoor spaces of buildings that connect to the lower part of buildings. Finally, from an urban design perspective, POPS connect the surrounding area and improve the cityscape. In all, POPS are co-produced public spaces that serve various functions in urban areas.

2.4.   Urban transformation as context

The previous sections provided an overview of the research topic, and this section describes the transitional context in which the research topic is embedded. Transformation is a broad term that is often used as a metaphor for societal change. Researchers and practitioners rely on vague definitions of transformational change. However, Iwaniec et al. (2019) distinguish between two types of transformation—unintentional and intentional—based on whether the outcome of an event is intended or not. Unintentional changes are often undesirable and unforeseen side effects that typically follow a disruptive event such as a war or natural disaster. The literature related to unintentional change examines how events transform a city or allow for transformation. In the scholarly literature, the dominant framing of unintentional transformation of cities focuses on forced transformation and mitigating undesirable changes or adapting to disturbances (Folke et al., 2010; Crépin et al., 2012). However, disruptive events can also create opportunities for intentional transformation. For example, the process of urbanisation involves multiple political, economic, and social drivers that can encourage local government, private investors, and reformers to promote and implement change in a city (Harvey, 2000). Such changes (e.g., toward economic growth, environmentally sustainable development, and social justice) can be classified as intentional transformations. The research examines public space in the context of both unintentional and intentional transformation. It not only examines how certain events or planned interventions produce unintended effects in relation to public space but also illustrates how cities may use such consequences as an opportunity for sharing their responsibility with other actors. The following paragraphs will provide a review of the literature related to two relevant contexts: rapid urbanisation and post-socialism.

The term "urbanisation" refers to the demographic process of shifting a country's population balance from rural to urban areas (Jenkins et al., 2007). Currently, half of the global population lives in cities; two-thirds of the world's population is predicted to live in urban areas by 2050 (United Nations, 2018). Migration to towns and cities may be motivated by several factors, including economic opportunities, education, disaster, famine, and war. Conventional economic theories of urbanisation and migration explain urban growth as a function of economic development, whereas traditional social theory emphasises push and pull factors (Jenkins et al., 2007). Urbanisation is not a new phenomenon, but it has increased significantly in the past 200 years since the Industrial Revolution.

The short and rapid history of industrialisation and subsequent urbanisation is a common pattern in East Asian countries. Many of these countries have reached a level of industrialisation in the past few decades that took countries in the West at least a century to reach (Miao, 2001). Accordingly, East Asian countries have seen both rapid urban expansion and population growth. The total urban land of the East Asia region grew from 106,000 square kilometres in 2000 to 135,000 square kilometres in 2010, and the total urban population of the region increased from 579 million in 2000 to 778 million in 2010 (World Bank Group, 2015). This rapid transition has had an enormous impact on the physical environment due to the increased number of people and their activities, as well as the increased demands on resources and services ranging from housing to transportation access. It is a daunting task for the public sector to provide a rapidly increasing population with sufficient resources and public services.

East Asian cities are also characterised by high population density. Large cities tend to attract additional population growth due to labour supplies, capital, and the concentration of infrastructure. In 2000, the urban population and population density of East Asian countries were denser than urban areas in other areas of the world, including Europe, Latin America, and North America (World Bank Group, 2015). The majority of urban areas in East Asia grew denser between 2000 and 2010. High population density, often coupled with high building density, has a strong influence on cities. Therefore, it is essential to understand the distribution and density of people in a city or country to ensure that appropriate resources and services are available where they are needed (Ritchie & Roser, 2018).

The trend of post-socialism also provides important context for this research. The political and economic transformation in Central and Eastern Europe following the fall of socialism has created a unique circumstance in time and space, and the influence of this transformation on urban space has provided ample opportunity for studies on urban transformation and urban planning in times of rapid changes. The most important post-socialist political changes include the revival of the multi-party system and free parliamentary elections. Another significant element of political transformation related to urban change is decentralisation. Important post-socialist economic transformations include the free flow of foreign capital investments and modern technology to Central and Eastern Europe (Kovács, 1999). As global corporations have expanded, the built environments of post-socialist cities have altered rapidly. Some neighbourhoods have experienced revitalization, whereas others have encountered social exclusion. Industrial areas have turned to ghost zones within months due to the closure of many state-run enterprises (Stanilov, 2007). Polarization and growing competition within the urban network of Eastern Europe have also impacted urban spaces. Cities, and particularly capital cities, have benefited from post-socialist urban transformation; however, other places such as socialist new towns and traditional industrial centres have suffered recessions as a result of these transformations.

Some scholars have argued that the recent urban restructuring has caused post-socialist cities to lose socialist features and acquire capitalist forms (Häussermann, 1996). This argument seems somewhat valid, because many of the problems and processes that have become typical in post-socialist cities in recent years also existed in Western Europe two or three decades earlier (Kovács, 1999). Hirt (2006) has argued that built forms in post-socialist cities have changed to become similar to forms in capitalist cities, but differences exist in the pace and intensity of these forms. Moreover, Hirt explains that the causes of urban restructuring differ between post-socialist and capitalist cities. In the post-socialist context, an economic downturn, a rapid withdrawal of the public sector from housing production, and the breakup of large state building firms have all contributed to urban restructuring. The situation also differs between cities in Central and Eastern Europe. For example, reunification has created a unique condition of urban transformation in Eastern Germany. A factor that differentiates urban restructuring in Germany from that of other post-socialist countries in Europe is the strong support provided by the western part of the unified Germany (Wießer, 1999).

The political and economic restructuring since 1989 has changed all facets of society, which has presented difficult challenges for urban planners. A revision of planning theory and practice was required. One distinct feature of planning in the post-socialist context was a weakened position of the public sector in urban planning (Hirt, 2014). Indeed, public-led planning acquired a negative connotation in the post-socialist world because it was considered a vestige of the communist system. Urban planners also encountered a lack of hard instruments of spatial planning, such as enforceable development plans. Inexperienced planning bureaucracy both in new legal framework and in negotiating with private investors allowed investors to realize their plans (Nuissl & Rink, 2005). Property rights were redefined in favour of private interests, which further limited the capacity of the government (Stanilov, 2007). Nuissl and Rink (2005) have argued that even if planners had had proper instruments, they would not have been able to withstand the pressure from investors, because politicians and planners saw the changing political landscape as an opportunity for their cities. In a climate dominated by a social imperative of deregulation and market liberalisation, the process of privatisation was celebrated as evidence of becoming "Western" (Stanilov, 2007; Hirt, 2014).

2.5. Conclusion

The aim of this chapter was to define public space and highlight its changing nature. Public space is a multi-dimensional concept characterised by a range of dimensions, including ownership, maintenance, accessibility, and inclusiveness. Public spaces are produced by and within a society; as society changes, they constantly evolve. Three characteristics of contemporary public space result from economic, sociocultural, and political shifts: (a) high-quality public space; (b) diverse and secured public space; and (c) co-produced public space. A fundamental goal of the literature review is to identify research gaps. Studies exist regarding the impact of societal shifts on public space in general; however, less is known about the impact of a transitional context on public space, during which societal changes are more dynamic in pace and intensity. The present book is intended to address this research gap.

Chapter 3. Research design and methodology

This chapter serves as an intermezzo between the theoretical and empirical parts of the book and elaborates on the methods employed to answer the four research questions presented in Chapter 1. The aim of this research is to investigate public space in a transitional context, specifically in relation to its provision and management. For an in-depth analysis, cases were selected based on two criteria: first, areas that have undergone radical changes, and second, areas that have since faced high development pressure. The reason for the second criterion is that areas with high development pressure are likely to change more rapidly due to high interest. Cases were sought especially in Seoul and Berlin for reasons of practicality: I have prior knowledge of both cities and the language skills to obtain the requisite data and subsequently produce high-quality qualitative research. Indeed, both cities fulfil criteria as they have a history of rapid change and high development pressure as the capital cities. Finding an appropriate case within both cities involved several steps. First, I read the relevant literature to identify possible cases in both cities. I then asked experts in the field to recommend cases. Having identified several possible cases in both cities, I screened these by way of site visits. Finally, Teheran-ro and Mediaspree area were selected.

Four research methods are used in case study research: comparative analysis, document analysis, expert interview, and site visit and analysis. In this study, multiple methods and sources of data are used for triangulation. Triangulation, first advocated by Todd Jick, allows for verification of results: 'The convergence or agreement between methods [...] enhances our belief that results are valid and not a methodological artifact' (Jick, 1979, 602). The specific methods used are explained in the following sections.

3.1. Comparative analysis

In recent years, there has been a revival of comparative methods and an ever-growing body of comparative studies (Krehl & Weck, 2020), including in urban and regional planning. Thus, it is important to conduct comparative research in a conscious manner. As Booth (2011) argues, 'the very first question that we need to confront is why we wish to undertake comparative research at all' (14). Recent studies have suggested two general reasons: 'the furtherance of explanatory and predictive theory, and the understanding and transfer of policy from one country to another' (Couch & Fraser, 2003, 7). Similarly, Faludi and Hamnett (1975) put forward three generic purposes for comparative planning research: the advancement of theory in planning; the improvement of planning practice; and the harmonisation of planning systems. Tilly (1984), meanwhile, distinguishes four types of comparative analysis based on purpose:

- Universalising comparison involves the use of comparison to develop theories
- Individualising comparison contrasts 'a small number of cases in order to grasp the uniqueness of each case' (82)
- Variation-finding comparison seeks to 'establish a principle of variation in the character or intensity of a phenomenon by examining systemic differences between instances' (82)
- Encompassing comparison 'places different instances at various locations within the same system on the way to explaining their characteristics as a function of their varying relationships to the system as a whole' (83).

Among these four types of comparative analysis, this research falls under individualising comparison. It contrasts planning instruments used for POPS in Teheran-ro and Mediaspree area and their outcomes (see Table 3.1) to grasp the uniqueness of the instruments used in each case. In fact, special characteristics can often only be seen in comparison. By examining two cases in depth, this study aims to broaden existing knowledge on the topic. Moreover, it aims to improve practice by informing policymakers on alternative policy approaches in case their cities encounter similar problems.

Table 3.1 Subjects of comparison

Category	Subcategory
Regulation of the provision of POPS	Zone, facility (building), location of POPS, type of POPS, number of POPS, dimension of POPS, signage, other amenities, indoor POPS, incentives
Regulation of the management of POPS	Maintenance of POPS, financial support, inspection of POPS, infraction proceedings, use of POPS
Outcomes of regulation	Maintenance (degree of cleanliness, provision of amenities, practice of control), accessibility (degree of physical and visual accessibility), inclusiveness (degree of types of activity)

Source: Author's own table.

International comparative urban research is challenging as each case is located in its unique historical and cultural setting; hence a number of literature that involve the comparison of global cases were carefully reviewed to set a framework (see e.g., Couch et al., 2003; Rubin, 2020). As shown in Table 3.1, this research focuses on how the public sector regulates POPS and with which planning instruments. This involves, on the one hand, regulation of the provision of POPS, including their location and type. On the other hand, public space requires some form of management after provision (Carmona et al., 2008; De Magalhães & Carmona, 2009). This applies to POPS as well, thus, regulation of the management of POPS is also examined. Management of POPS comprises five different aspects. First, it refers to maintenance and the implied routines that make POPS useable, clean and safe. This also ensures that the amenities within POPS are kept to desired standards. Second, management involves securing financial resources for said maintenance. Management also includes inspection (third) and infraction proceedings (fourth) to check whether POPS comply with arrangements. Fifth, management incorporates how POPS should be used and how conflicts between uses should be resolved. All these aspects regarding regulation of the provision and management of POPS are partly drawn from the preceding study by Park and Yang (2016). It should also be noted here that while analysing documents, further aspects were added to cover the full spectrum.

Lastly, the outcome of regulation of POPS provision and management is compared based on three criteria – maintenance, accessibility and inclusiveness – taken from the literature review. A number of POPS in both Teheran-ro and Mediaspree area are studied for comparison.

3.2.   Document analysis

Document analysis refers to 'a systemic procedure for reviewing or evaluating documents – both printed and electronic material' (Bowen, 2009, 27). Here, documents were used as sources of information for the empirical research. The first step of the research involved gathering secondary data from, among others, academic literature, legislation and planning documents related to the cases (see Appendix A). Document analysis was chosen for four reasons: (a) documents provided background information as well as historical insight into the cases; (b) they suggested questions that needed to be asked as part of the research; (c) they provided relevant research data; and (d) they provided verification of findings from other data sources.

One advantage of document analysis is accessibility since many documents are in the public domain. However, they often do not have sufficient detail to answer specific research questions. Hence, document analysis was used here in combination with other research methods, as described in the following sections.

3.3.   Expert interview

In addition to document analysis, semi-structured interviews with key actors were conducted because 'people are important data sources who have [...] knowledge and who can report on what happened, and why it happened' (Farthing, 2016, 201). Interview questions were designed, and respondents were selected and invited to the interview. In most cases, I contacted interviewees directly. For instance, I approached planning officers who are either responsible for POPS in Teheran-ro or Mediaspree area or who have sufficient knowledge of the relevant planning instruments. Researchers were selected based on their previous authorship of research studies on POPS in South Korea or Germany. In some cases, interviewees also suggested other names to contact. In total, 17 interviews were conducted: 16 face-to-face interviews and one written interview. Thirteen interviews out of 17 were conducted in Seoul; the remaining four took place in Berlin. This is partly due to the high number of documents available on the Mediaspree area. Interviews were conducted in Korean in Seoul and in German in Berlin.

Interviewees included planning officers, an architect, researchers, a building manager and an activist (see Appendix B). The key participants confirmed the findings and provided additional data that could not be found in the documents. For instance, planning officers whose daily routines include implementing planning instruments for POPS in Teheran-ro and Mediaspree area explained which planning instruments had been used where and why. Other planning officers coming from other districts or cities explained more about the planning instruments for POPS per se. An architect, a building manager and an activist from an NGO were also interviewed to hear their experiences of creating and maintaining POPS. Researchers gave a piece of advice for conducting an empirical research in Seoul and Berlin. To respect confidentiality and anonymity, the names and positions of respondents are not shown.

3.4.   Site visit and analysis

Site visit and analysis is a method dedicated to the study of a specific site (White, 1983). To better understand the planning instruments employed in both cases and their consequences, POPS were visited, analysed and evaluated. Four key dimensions of the publicness of public space were drawn from the literature review: ownership, maintenance, accessibility and inclusiveness. Ownership is not considered in this research since all of the selected POPS are privately owned. For the remaining three dimensions, an empirical model through which POPS can be evaluated is established (see Table 3.2). This model is hence based on a multifaceted interpretation of public space.

As already elaborated in the literature review, maintenance involves cleanliness, provision of amenities and practice of control. Whether a space is clean can be experienced, for example, through provision of adequate waste-collection facilities and the clearance of litter, fly tipping or fly posting. Provision of amenities, and how wide-ranging these amenities are, is also decisive. In turn, practice of control refers to the purpose of this control rather than its mere presence. As discussed in the literature review, the presence of control itself does not reduce the publicness of public space. Thus, what is examined is whether the practice of control aims to prevent anti-social behaviour only; if so, it is seen positively.

Table 3.2 Operationalisation of a model for evaluating POPS

Criteria	Indicator	Scale		
Mainte-nance	Degree of cleanliness	1=low	2= medium	3=high
	Degree of provision of amenities	1=low	2=medium	3=high
	Degree of practice of control	1=high	2=medium	3=low
Accessibility	Degree of physical accessibility	1=low	2=medium	3=high
	Degree of visual accessibility	1=low	2=medium	3=high
Inclusive-ness	Degree of types of activity	1=low	2=medium	3=high

Source: Author's own table.

Accessibility is about both physical and visual accessibility, which can be measured through the presence of a gate or fence, for instance. Another crucial factor is whether a space has barrier-free pavements or is well connected to the adjacent street. Lastly, inclusiveness considers whether various activities can be accommodated so that a space can be used by all, regardless of gender, age, race or disability. It is also dependent on the other two criteria: the better POPS are maintained and accessible, the more likely they are to attract diverse groups. The size of POPS is also important: the larger the POPS, the more likely it is to accommodate different uses.

Each indicator has three discrete scales. This model does not represent an improvement on the models of measuring the publicness of public space introduced in Chapter 2, but is intended as a pragmatic research tool for this research.

The research concentrated on four locations in Teheran-ro and four in Mediaspree area (see Appendix C). POPS in Teheran-ro were selected from three blocks near the Seolleung underground station. When selecting POPS for detailed study, I aimed to incorporate a wide range of POPS both in terms of year of their creation and type. Hence, POPS from 1999 to 2010 were selected. Four types of POPS out of the five identified in the Seoul POPS provision guidelines (City of Seoul, 2015) were selected. These include pedestrian space, garden, plaza and pioti/sunken. POPS in Mediaspree area were selected according to the availability of explanatory statements due to the amount of information provided. In other words, areas that have established a B-Plan were selected.

POPS in Teheran-ro were visited several times in June 2017 for analysis according to the three aforementioned dimensions. Notes and photographs were taken. Each site was visited several times on weekdays and on weekends between 7 a.m. and 11 p.m. POPS in Mediaspree area were visited three times – in November 2017 plus May and July in 2018. Notes and photographs were taken; the latter are presented in Chapter 7. At this point, it is important to note that the number of people shown in the photos does not signify whether the POPS are actively used. In most cases, I have purposefully used photos where either no one is present or no faces are recognisable due to the issue of portrait rights and privacy.

It is also important to note that I measured the quality of POPS as physical spaces and not necessarily how they are used in reality. Given that the quality of a space is certainly related to its use, I assumed that the better POPS are maintained, accessible and inclusive, the more they will be used. That said, I was aware that certain spaces that are poorly accessible and less equipped may be even more actively used than fully designed and programmed spaces. Also, spaces may be experienced differently by users depending on their gender, age, and so on. However, such matters lie beyond the scope of this research. Nevertheless, when visiting each POPS, I stayed for five to 30 minutes to gain some personal impressions on how the POPS were being used – this may partly flow in the evaluation, especially for inclusiveness. The scale from one to three is by no means an absolute figure here; for example, three points in cleanliness does not mean that a POPS is absolutely clean. It should be understood as a relative figure when comparing the outcome of POPS planning instruments.

3.5.   Conclusion

In this chapter, the formulated research questions were translated into practical instruments that can generate answers (operationalisation). Multiple methods and sources of data are used for triangulation. Table 3.3 illustrates which method is used for what purpose. This chapter also described each of the methods employed, gave justification for why each was used, and explained how it was used.

Table 3.3 Research questions and methods used

Research questions	Methods used	Chapter
What challenges does the public sector face in providing and managing public space in a transitional context?	Document analysis	See Chapter 4
How does the public sector address these challenge?	Document analysis Expert interview	See Chapter 5 and 6
What do the outcomes of the respective planning instruments look like in reality?	Document analysis Expert interview Site visit and analysis	See Chapter 7
What implications does the research provide for cities undergoing rapid transformation and facing high development pressure, and which are looking for ways to engage other stakeholders, including the private sector, in public space provision and management?	Comparative analysis	See Chapter 8

Source: Author's own table.

Before moving to the next chapter, I would like to address the limitations of this research. First, there is an imbalance in the presentation of the information, especially in Chapter 7. This is mainly due to the different amounts of accessible information. For instance, the documents called explanatory statements for Mediaspree area provided a large amount of information for each case of POPS in the area on which I could elaborate. However, no such documentation exists for POPS in Teheran-ro or in South Korea in general. As a result, a gap in terms of the amount of information available on each POPS was identified. Although I tried to close this gap by carrying out more expert interviews in Seoul, I have to admit to inconstancy in parts. From another viewpoint, this point illustrates the difference in characteristics between planning instruments used in Teheran-ro and Mediaspree area: while planning instruments are used case-by-case for POPS in Mediaspree area, meaning each POPS has its own story to tell, this is not the case in Teheran-ro, where the same regulation is applied to all POPS.

Another limitation is that the evaluation of POPS may have been influenced by my own subjective feelings. As an example, how I perceived a sense of control may be totally different from the perception of others. Whether smoking is allowed is another example; whereas smokers see permission positively, non-smokers are against it. What is more, personal impressions can easily be affected by factors such as time of day, seasons and weather. Nonetheless, the site visit and analysis helped me to understand and interpret the uniqueness of planning instruments in both cases more effectively, as well as their respective strengths and weaknesses.

Lastly, given the limited number of case studies, the findings cannot be generalised. However, the intention is not to generalise but to identify uniqueness of planning instruments. The findings provide an initial overview of planning instruments that are relevant to the provision and management of POPS in each case and support the development of a number of key recommendations in the field.

Chapter 4. Challenges of providing and managing public space in a transitional context

In response to the first research question, this chapter considers the cases of Teheran-ro in Seoul and Mediaspree area in Berlin in terms of the challenges faced by the public sector in providing and managing public space in a transitional context. This chapter is informed by a document analysis.

4.1. Teheran-ro, Seoul

The Korean War (1950–1953) severely damaged Seoul, South Korea's capital. As a result, the role of urban planning was to restore the city and to cater to a rapidly growing population (Kim et al., 2001; City of Seoul, n.d.). The post-war period, and in particular between the early 1960s and the mid-1970s, deserves to be called the most dynamic period in Korean urban history since the urban population growth rate was very high. Seoul was no exception: the city experienced rapid urbanisation followed by industrialisation. Within 15 years, the population almost tripled from 2.3 million in 1960 to 6.8 million in 1975; it reached 10 million in 1988 (PopulationStat, 2020). As the concentration of population in Seoul continued to accelerate, the city's area expanded from 268 to 605 square kilometres in 1963 (Youn & Jung, 2009).

In the process, Gangnam[1] was incorporated into Seoul (Kang, 2015). Gangnam, which had been farmland until the 1960s, was developed as the very first new town project following Korean independence. The urban structure in

---

1   Gangnam literally means the area on the south side of Han River in Seoul. Its administrative border has been changed several times during its development. Here, the analysis refers to the present-day Gangnam and Seocho districts.

Gangnam was formed through a series of steps that started with the first proposal in 1962 (Youn & Jung, 2009). Superblock concepts, a ring-radial roadway circulation system, grid-pattern streets and riverside roads were discussed and partly adopted. In addition, apartment complexes started to be built in the late 1970s to remedy the shortage of housing and improve the efficiency of land use (Kang et al., 1999). Gangnam thus transformed into one of the most affluent areas within Seoul and in South Korea as a whole. Below, the case of Teheran-ro will be analysed to discover the effects of urbanisation on public space provision and management.

Teheran-ro is one of the main roads in Gangnam. In its development, Heo (2011) distinguishes four major periods: foundation, preparation, promotion, and expansion. During the foundation period, the character of Teheran-ro was determined as a main road forming superblocks through a land readjustment project. In the next phase, an urban design was established to provide the basis for the development of large buildings along Teheran-ro. During this period, a subway line opened along Teheran-ro ahead of the 1986 Asian Games and the 1988 Seoul Olympics. The actual development of the road started between 1987 and 1997, accompanied by full-scale developments of office buildings. In the last phase, other types of buildings were built on the remaining land, and the development of the area was almost complete. Within just 20 years, Teheran-ro had become one of the most densely populated areas for office buildings in Seoul.

In Teheran-ro, the rapid development of high-rise buildings meant that the quality of the urban environment worsened (Kang et al., 2009). In fact, no emphasis was placed on the quality of the urban environment, although it is directly linked to urban life (Kim & Kim, 2011). Pedestrians lacked space to walk or rest along Teheran-ro. To prevent reckless development, it became necessary to manage individual buildings by providing development guidelines for the use and location of buildings, exterior spaces and parking lots, to name a few. Gangnam and Teheran-ro also faced the challenge of rapidly increasing land value due to the high development pressure. In fact, the official land value for not only residential but also commercial areas in Gangnam district is the highest in Seoul (The Seoul Research Data Service, n.d.), and land value in Teheran-ro is especially high. Hence, it is too costly for the public sector to acquire land or to provide and maintain public space in the area without external support. In other words, public sector is incapable of providing and managing public space alone.

4.2.   Mediaspree area, Berlin

Germany's capital city has a complicated history, not least due to its Cold War division. Berlin underwent radical change after the fall of socialism and the subsequent reunification in 1989. The political and economic restructuring after 1989 changed all facets of society, including the established structures of planning. In the following section, Mediaspree area will be examined to identify which challenges transformation has brought about in the provision and management of public space.

Mediaspree is one of the largest property investment projects in Berlin. The project area is situated in the southeast of Berlin, along both sides of the river Spree (3.7 kilometres in length), and covers a section of 180 hectares (Ahlfeldt, 2010). For the most part, the site is located within the district of Friedrichshain-Kreuzberg. The area had already been an important industrial area before the Second World War; during the Cold War, the riverfront was divided into border zones (with the border drawn in the middle of the river itself). Accessibility to both sides of the river continued to be limited, as the East side was used for railway and harbour facilities and the West side mainly for trade and industry (Hofmann, 2018). The area went through a radical transformation in the post-unification period. The once unattractive industrial area has since become a world-renowned hotspot for alternative music culture as numerous industrial facilities along the river fell into disuse and opened up to new uses (Ahlfeldt, 2010).

The area was soon recognised as an essential development area due to its central location and fertile cultural environment, as well as the boom in waterfront development projects in other metropolises (Dohnke, 2014). In light of the city's difficult financial situation as well as the social imperative for deregulation and market liberalisation, this development was expected to come from the private sector. As a result, Berlin used marketing and incentive strategies to draw investment; initial plans were made as early as the mid-1990s, the aim of which was to bring positive economic impetus to the area by establishing media and creative industries and implementing an urban renewal of the surrounding area (Ahlfeldt, 2010). A dozen high-rise buildings, an arena for large events, other event locations, and several hundred thousand square metres of offices, hotels and luxury apartments were planned. To realise this mega-project, the vast majority of land that belonged to the city of Berlin or to public enterprises, especially in the former East Berlin, was privatised by means of selling it to the highest bidder, with subsequent development by private actors (Dohnke, 2014).

The vision of the development project stood in sharp contrast to the reality of life in the adjacent neighbourhoods, which were generally inhabited by people with low incomes (Dohnke, 2014). Among them, there was increasing concern over the eventual adverse effects of the project in the neighbourhoods, including gentrification. Alarmed by the coming changes, a citizens' protest initiative called *Mediaspree Versenken!* (Sink Mediaspree) was formed in 2007 around three core demands: (a) no new buildings on a 50-metre-wide strip on both sides of the river Spree; (b) no new buildings between Stadtbahn and Köpenicker/Schlesische Straße; and (c) a new pedestrian and cyclist bridge over the river instead of another road bridge (Bezirksamt FHKR von Berlin, 2009a). The movement initiated a referendum, *Spreeufer für Alle* (Spree riverbank for all), in 2008; with a turnout of 18.6%, almost 86% of voters approved the initiative (Bezirksamt FHKR von Berlin, 2009a). Although the result of the referendum was not legally binding, it was taken seriously by the district office due to the public pressure (Hofmann, 2018). A special committee was established in the district parliament; yet, it did not have any great success. An amendment of the plans was made on state-owned properties only.

The Mediaspree area has been a construction site for many years (Hofmann, 2018). In the mid-to-late 1990s, the office towers Trias (1996), the Twin-tower (1997), the Jannowitz-Centre (1997), the Treptowers (1998) and the IBIS Hotel (2000) were completed. In the 2000s, Osthafen witnessed the inflow of corporations, mainly from the media and creative industries. In 2002, for example, Universal Music moved its headquarters from Hamburg to the converted Eierkühlhaus in Mediaspree area; this was followed by new developments for MTV Deutschland (2007), Fernsehwerft (2009), Labels 2 (2009) and nhow Design Hotel (2010). In 2013, the Coca-Cola Deutschland headquarters was moved to the area. A residential building The White was also built, and there has been a development boost in the area around the Mercedes-Benz Arena as well, with office, commercial and residential buildings as well as a hotel planned.

The transformative influx of foreign investment, along with the rapid privatisation of state-owned properties (especially in the former East Berlin), resulted in enormous changes to public space in Mediaspree area. Given that a considerable amount of the riverside was to remain privately owned, securing public access to the riverside became a matter of concern, as public access could be denied by private landowners seeking to discourage undesirable visitors and disruptive forms of use. More generally, the provision of public space in this rapidly changing context was an issue due to the amount of new development planned in the neighbourhood. However, the public sector was unwilling to (re)purchase properties in response to public demand (Dohnke, 2014). Even though the Senate Department for Urban Development and Environment and the district office[2] played a central role, austerity measures meant they were unable to contribute to a larger extent (Hofmann, 2018). Private investors and developers came to the forefront with their resources, while civil society had their own visions; ultimately, it was collaborative efforts between the public sector and relevant economic and civil society actors that proved essential to addressing the challenges of public space provision and management.

4.3. Conclusion

This chapter attempted to answer the first research question, identifying the challenges faced by the public sector in providing and managing public space in a transitional context in both Teheran-ro in Seoul and Mediaspree area in Berlin. The findings suggest that public space provision and management are profoundly affected when cities undergo radical transformation. The document analysis revealed that although the drivers of transformation in each case are different, they arrive at the same outcome, whereby the public sector is incapable of providing and managing public space alone, especially in times of change.

The challenges observed in Teheran-ro and Mediaspree area are remarkable due to the pace and intensity of change in both areas. The rapid development of Teheran-ro as part of urban expansion and population growth meant that the quality of the urban environment worsened. Although public spaces were necessary to provide adequate walking space and resting areas and to prevent reckless development, the surge in land value meant it became too costly to buy land for public space. Mediaspree area, meanwhile,

---

2   Berlin has a two-level government system: the Senate and Districts. District offices in Berlin are a relevant decentralised part of the administration of Berlin (Bezirksämter). They have considerable powers. They also have a district mayor, who is the head of the administration, elected by a council. There are 12 district mayors; they also form a council together with the mayor of Berlin.

witnessed radical changes in the aftermath of German reunification: securing open space along the riverside and providing public space within the neighbourhood were significant issues, yet the public sector was neither willing to nor capable of (re)purchasing private land. In conclusion, both Teheran-ro and Mediaspree area demonstrate that common issues around public space arise when cities undergo radical transformation and face intense development pressure.

Chapter 5. Planning instruments for POPS in Teheran-ro, Seoul

The previous chapter highlighted how, even though the drivers of transformation in each case are different, both were faced with the same challenge: public sector's incapacity to provide and manage public space without external support, especially in times of change. The question now arises: How does the public sector react to this challenge?

Several instruments have been used in Teheran-ro to engage the private sector and provide public space in the form of POPS (see Table 5.1). In the following sections, each instrument will be analysed in response to the second research question.

Table 5.1 Planning instruments for POPS in Teheran-ro

Direct planning instruments	Formal planning instruments at national level	Building Act
		Presidential Decree of Building Act
		National Land Planning and Utilisation Act
		Presidential Decree of National Land Planning and Utilisation Act
	Formal planning instruments at city level	Seoul Metropolitan Government Ordinance on Building
		Guideline for Seoul District Unit Planning
		2025 Seoul Basic Plan of Maintenance and Improvement of Urban Areas
	Informal planning instruments at city level	Seoul Building Review Standard
		Seoul POPS Provision Guideline

Source: Author's own table.

5.1.   Formal planning instrument at national level

All POPS in South Korea are provided within a legal framework implemented at the national level. In this section, two relevant Acts and their Presidential Decrees for POPS are analysed.

5.1.1.   Building Act and its Presidential Decree

The purposes of the Building Act are to 'improve the safety, functions, environment and view of buildings and to promote public welfare by establishing the standards for and purposes of use of sites, structures and facilities of buildings'.[1] In addition, its Presidential Decree is intended to 'prescribe matters delegated by the Building Act as well as those necessary for its enforcement'.[2]

The Building Act went through complete revision in 1991 with an aim to promote safety and public welfare, such as fire prevention and sanitation, within buildings (Park & Yang, 2016). As part of the revision, a clause on POPS was first established in consideration of the impact of large-scale buildings on urban space. The Presidential Decree of the Building Act and the Seoul Metropolitan Government Ordinance on Building were adjusted in 1992 and 1993, respectively to institutionalise POPS (Park & Yang, 2016). The Building Act and its Presidential Decree provide regulation on POPS, including provision, maintenance, inspection and infraction proceedings. While the Building Act provides a general framework, its Presidential Decree provides more detailed regulation.

The Building Act states in which zone POPS shall be provided to create a pleasant urban environment. These include: 'a general residential zone, a quasi-residential zone, a commercial zone, a quasi-industrial zone and an area designated and publicly notified by the Special Self-Governing City Mayor, the Special Self-Governing Province Governor or the head of a city/town/district that is highly anticipated to be urbanised'.[3]

Within these zones, POPS shall be provided on the site of any of the following facilities whose total floor area exceeds 5,000 square metres for relevant use: 'cultural or assembly facilities, religious facilities, sales facilities, trans-

---

1   Article 1 of Building Act.
2   Article 1 of Presidential Decree of Building Act.
3   Article 43 (1) of Building Act.

portation facilities, business facilities, lodging facilities or other facilities for public use determined by an Ordinance on Building'.[4]

As a rule, owners of the buildings involved must provide POPS. The size of POPS shall be 'prescribed by a city's Ordinance on Building – within 10% of the area of the relevant site'.[5] When creating POPS, owners should ensure that nothing blocks access to the site.[6] In addition, 'amenities prescribed by an Ordinance on Building, such as benches or pergolas, should be installed for greater convenience of use and in an environmentally friendly manner'.[7]

Both the Building Act and its Presidential Decree point to incentives, which shall be given to owners of the respective buildings for providing POPS. These incentives are given based on the size of the POPS. In cases where POPS are installed, regulations on building-to-land ratio, floor area ratio and height limit may be relaxed.[8] In addition, the owners of buildings that are not subject to the provision of POPS shall receive incentives if they provide POPS.[9]

Based on the Building Act, POPS are maintained by building owners in compliance with the relevant standards.[10] Where there are multiple owners within a building, a managing body makes decisions over, for example, maintenance of POPS (Interviewee 8). As buildings with POPS are generally large in size, they typically feature a management office for building managers (Interviewee 8). Building managers are those individuals who carry out maintenance work and are either hired directly or contracted out.

While building owners are responsible for the maintenance of POPS, the public sector is responsible for an annual inspection of the maintenance and management of POPS and for establishing and deploying a maintenance plan for corrective measures.[11] For systematic follow-up, a management register is kept for any buildings in violation of the law.[12] Owners of these buildings

---

4   Article 27-2 (1) of Presidential Decree of Building Act.
5   Article 27-2 (2) of Presidential Decree of Building Act.
6   Article 27-2 (3) 2 of Presidential Decree of Building Act.
7   Article 27-2 (3) 3 of Presidential Decree of Building Act.
8   Article 43 (2) of Building Act.
9   Article 27-2 (5) of Presidential Decree of Building Act.
10 Article 35 (1) of Building Act and Article 23 of Presidential Decree of Building Act.
11 Article 115 (1) of Presidential Decree of Building Act.
12 Article 115 (2) of Presidential Decree of Building Act.

are required to make corrections within a given period; if not fulfilled by the given deadline, a penalty is imposed.[13]

Furthermore, the Presidential Decree states that cultural or promotional events for residents may be held on POPS for up to 60 days in a year, as long as they do not hinder public use.[14]

5.1.2. National Land Planning and Utilisation Act and its Presidential Decree

The purpose of the National Land Planning and Utilisation Act (hereafter National Land Planning Act) is to 'promote public welfare and to improve quality of life by supporting the formulation and implementation of plans to utilise, develop and preserve national land'.[15] The purpose of its Presidential Decree is to 'provide for matters delegated by the National Land Planning Act and matters necessary to implement the Act'.[16]

The National Land Planning Act and its Presidential Decree provide regulation on incentives for POPS in District Unit Planning zones. District Unit Planning (hereafter DUP) is 'an urban management plan whose purpose is to rationalise land use, to increase its functionality, to improve visual aesthetics, to secure a better environment and to manage the relevant area in a systematic and planned manner'.[17] In cases where an individual who intends to construct a building in a DUP zone has installed POPS in excess of the liable area, the floor area ratio and height limits applicable to the building may be relaxed.[18]

5.2. Formal planning instruments at city level

In accordance with the legal framework provided at the national level, each municipality creates its own formal planning instruments for POPS. The first of these is the Seoul Metropolitan Government Ordinance on Building, which

---

13   Article 80 (1) of Building Act.

14   Article 27-2 (6) of Presidential Decree of Building Act.

15   Article 1 of National Land Planning and Utilisation Act.

16   Article 1 of Presidential Decree of National Land Planning and Utilisation Act.

17   Article 2 of National Land Planning and Utilisation Act.

18   Article 46 (3) of Presidential Decree of National Land Planning and Utilisation Act.

is an ordinance of the Building Act. The second is the Guideline for Seoul District Unit Planning, which is a statutory instrument under the National Land Planning Act. The third is the 2025 Seoul Basic Plan of Maintenance and Improvement of Urban Areas. Those areas where either the Guideline for Seoul District Unit Planning or the 2025 Seoul Basic Plan of Maintenance and Improvement of Urban Areas is applied must also take the Seoul Metropolitan Government Ordinance on Building into account. In areas where both are applied, all three standards should be taken into consideration. In areas that do not fall under either of these two plans, only the Seoul Metropolitan Government Ordinance on Building applies (Park & Yang, 2016). These three formal instruments are analysed in greater depth in the following section.

5.2.1.   Seoul Metropolitan Government Ordinance on Building

The purpose of the Seoul Metropolitan Government Ordinance on Building (hereafter Seoul Ordinance on Building) is 'to provide for matters delegated by, among others, the Building Act and its Presidential Decree and matters necessary to their implementation'.[19] Having been amended several times since 1993, it has taken increasingly concrete shape.

In accordance with the Building Act and its Presidential Decree, the Seoul Ordinance on Building lists facilities that should provide POPS if their total floor area exceeds 5,000 square metres. These include: 'cultural or assembly facilities, sales facilities, business facilities, lodging facilities, medical facilities, sports facilities, amusement facilities, religious facilities, transport facilities, and funeral halls'.[20]

The Seoul Ordinance on Building prescribes the size of POPS at up to 10% of the total site area. More specifically, the Ordinance states as follows: '(a) if the total floor area is greater than 5,000 and less than 10,000 square metres, 5% of the site area shall be used for POPS; (b) if the total floor area is greater than 10,000 and less than 30,000 square metres, 7% of the site area shall be used for POPS; and (c) if the total floor area exceeds 30,000 square metres, 10% of the site area shall be used for POPS'.[21] The Seoul Ordinance on Building further lists a set of standards on how POPS should be created (see Table 5.2).

---

19   Article 1 of Seoul Metropolitan Government Ordinance on Building.
20   Article 26 (1) 1 of Seoul Metropolitan Government Ordinance on Building.
21   Article 26 (1) 2 of Seoul Metropolitan Government Ordinance on Building.

Table 5.2 Standard for providing POPS in Seoul

Location	POPS should be created on the widest roadside that abuts the building site – one side of the building site shall abut more than one quarter of the roadside – and allows convenient general access. (Article 26 [2] 1) It should be created in the form of a small park in harmony with the street environment. (Article 26 [2] 1) In cases where it is unreasonable to create such a space on the widest roadside, the location may be determined individually after consideration by the committee. (Article 26 [2] 1) POPS shall be created at ground level but may, after consideration by the committee, be built underground if it is open and can be used by the public. (Article 26 [2] 7)
Number	POPS shall not be divided into more than two spaces, each of which shall be larger than 45 square metres. (Article 26 [2] 2)
Dimension	POPS shall not be less than five metres in width. (Article 26 [2] 3) In case of piloti structures, the minimum height shall be six metres. (Article 26 [2] 4)
Signage	Among the different amenities, the provision of clear, visible and readable signage is essential to identify POPS as public spaces and to provide useful information (e.g., amenities provided, hours of access). Hence, more than one plaque shall be installed at its entrance in accordance with the relevant standards. (Article 26 [2] 6)
Other amenities	Amenities for the comfort of the general public shall be provided, such as landscaping, benches, pergolas, clock towers, fountains, outdoor stages and small public restrooms. (Article 26 [2] 5)

Source: Author's own table based on the Seoul Ordinance on Building.

Incentives are given based on the total size of the POPS. Whereas previous incentives were only given to POPS in excess of the liable area, this regulation has recently been changed (Interviewee 10). Now, incentives are given in line with the size of POPS installed and is calculated using a mathematical formula. Floor area ratio or height or a combination of both may then be relaxed accordingly.[22]

As regulated by the Building Act and its Presidential Decree, building owners are responsible for the maintenance of POPS. However, a mayor may support part of the necessary expenses in cases where POPS that are at least five years old are to be remodelled or subject to expert inspection.[23]

---

22   Article 26 (3) of Seoul Metropolitan Government Ordinance on Building.
23   Article 26 (4) 1 & 2 of Seoul Metropolitan Government Ordinance on Building.

In accordance with the Presidential Decree, the city of Seoul establishes its own inspection plan and conducts the inspection accordingly. A building owner who has created a POPS must submit a management register at the time of applying for approval for use of POPS.[24] As a rule, each district checks and manages POPS at least once a year.[25] Experts can be commissioned to 'conduct an inspection of the status and utilisation of POPS at least once every two years'.[26] If POPS are found to be in violation of the law, a penalty is imposed.[27]

The Seoul Ordinance on Building also declares that cultural or promotional events for residents may be held in POPS for up to 60 days in a year, given that they do not hinder public use.[28] Event details, such as the scope of the event, related procedure, hours of use and rules of conduct, shall be determined individually by the respective mayor.[29] In fact, the city of Seoul issued the criteria for the use of POPS in 2017: possible event types include exhibitions, concerts and markets, among others. Furthermore, it outlines compliance details on erecting facilities and noise levels (City of Seoul, 2017). In terms of process, the potential user is required to apply at least 14 days prior to the event to the relevant district office. The office then reviews the application, taking into account the character of the event and whether it would cause any inconvenience or danger to other pedestrians (Interviewee 3). If decision-making proves difficult, the district may ask committee members to review the application (Interviewee 3). Once a positive decision is made, the district contacts the relevant building owner and seeks agreement if approval was not given prior to the submission.

5.2.2. Guideline for Seoul District Unit Planning

The Guideline for Seoul District Unit Planning (hereafter Seoul DUP Guideline) is a statutory instrument under the National Land Planning Act. It provides guidance for POPS located within DUP areas in Seoul. The Guideline defines POPS as 'vacant lots within building sites that are open to the public

---

24   Article 26 (2) 8 of Seoul Metropolitan Government Ordinance on Building.
25   Article 26 (2) 8 of Seoul Metropolitan Government Ordinance on Building.
26   Article 26 (2) 9 of Seoul Metropolitan Government Ordinance on Building.
27   Article 45 of Seoul Metropolitan Government Ordinance on Building.
28   Article 26 (5) of Seoul Metropolitan Government Ordinance on Building.
29   Article 26 (5) of Seoul Metropolitan Government Ordinance on Building.

at all times for citizens' walking, resting as well as for continuous creation of green spaces in private land in order to create a pleasant environment in the area' (City of Seoul, 2016b, 87). It distinguishes three types of POPS: open type, sunken type and piloti type. Moreover, it prescribes the location of POPS. Aside from the type and location, the Guideline states how POPS should be created including number of POPS, dimension of POPS and amenities. Detailed guideline of each aspect of POPS is presented in Table 5.3. Lastly, it mentions incentives. The maximum incentive is 1.2 x floor area ratio or 1.2 x height (City of Seoul, 2016b). Unlike the Seoul Ordinance on Building, the Guideline states that incentives can be given either for floor area ratio or height, but the combination of both is not permitted. Moreover, incentives are applied to POPS exceeding the liable area, not to the total area of POPS.

Table 5.3 Guideline for providing POPS located within DUP areas in Seoul (Part I)

Type	Open type refers to outdoor POPS located adjacent to sidewalks and main roads. Sunken-type POPS are outdoor POPS at a lower level than the surrounding area, which allow public use at all times in connection with facilities like subway stations. Piloti-type POPS are outdoor POPS that also contain structures that support the loads of columns. (p. 88)
Location	POPS should be created on the widest roadside that abuts the building site while allowing for convenient general access. In cases where it is unreasonable to create such a space on the widest roadside, the location may be determined individually. In addition to the relationship with the adjacent land, the road network, main road, main sidewalk, and green axis within the DUP zone should also be considered. Each POPS should be created at ground-floor level so that it can be easily accessed by the public at all times. POPS should be created in a way that they connect well to one another. Sunken-type POPS may also be created; in this case, it is recommended that the POPS remain open 24/7. POPS should be located where a minimum amount of sunshine can be obtained. POPS in the form of plazas may be placed in front of the building. POPS should be planned in a way that can support various activities to activate those who use the street. (pp. 91-92)
Number	POPS should be connected to the street and created in one place to increase continuity and usability of the resting area. (p. 92)

Table 5.3 Guideline for providing POPS located within DUP areas in Seoul (Part II)

Dimension	In the case of piloti structures, the minimum height should be six metres. (p. 92)
Other amenities	Amenities such as landscaping, benches, pergolas, clock towers, fountains, outdoor stages and small public restrooms should be installed. Pavement material and pattern should have continuity with the pavement of the adjacent street. (p. 92)

Source: Author's own table based on the Seoul DUP Guideline.

5.2.3.   2025 Seoul Basic Plan of Maintenance and Improvement of Urban Areas

The 2025 Seoul Basic Plan of Maintenance and Improvement of Urban Areas (hereafter Seoul Basic Plan) is a long-term urban plan set out every 10 years. It distinguishes between outdoor and indoor POPS. The Plan defines outdoor POPS as 'public spaces created in private land for a pleasant local environment. They are open to the general public at all times' (City of Seoul, 2016a, 159). On the other hand, the Plan defines indoor POPS as 'open spaces with a public character inside buildings' (City of Seoul, 2016a, 159). In order to ensure that indoor POPS function as public spaces, continuity of space inside and outside the building should be taken into account. Moreover, the Plan requires indoor POPS to be visually transparent, barrier-free and open at least between 7 a.m. and 10 p.m. The Plan addresses a number of aspects, thereby providing a guideline for both types of POPS in Seoul (see Table 5.4 and 5.5).

The Plan states that incentives can be given for creating indoor POPS, but only with respect to relaxing floor area ratio (not height limit) (City of Seoul, 2016a).

Table 5.4 Guideline for providing outdoor POPS located within Seoul Basic Plan areas in Seoul

Number	POPS should not be divided unless the resulting sections are larger than 45 square metres. (p. 173)
Location	POPS should be created in consideration of the POPS of surrounding buildings and other outdoor spaces so that it can be connected and integrated with streets and existing parks. (p. 173)
Signage	At least one signage should be installed where users can easily see it (e.g., at the entrance). Signage should indicate that the space is POPS, provide a layout of the POPS and the amenities available, as well as opening hours, house rules, and the names and contact information of the owner and building manager. Design should be in accordance with the standards of each district. (p. 173)

Source: Author's own table based on the Seoul Basic Plan.

Table 5.5 Guideline for providing indoor POPS located within Seoul Basic Plan areas in Seoul

Dimension	The minimum width, height and size for indoor POPS are six metres, nine metres and 330 square metres, respectively. The entrance used to access an indoor POPS shall be at least six metres in width. (p. 176)
Location	POPS should be created in consideration of the POPS of surrounding buildings and other outdoor spaces so that it can be connected and integrated with streets and existing parks. (p. 175)
Signage	Signage is required to be placed in a place that is easily recognisable to citizens, including at the entrance, to indicate that the space is a POPS. It should also include the following: layout of POPS, background history of POPS, opening hours, house rules, and names and contact information of owner and building manager. (p. 176)
Other amenities	Within the building itself, small commercial amenities (such as kiosks) may be provided along with other amenities like fountains or landscaping. Chairs and tables should be installed for citizens to rest and should be indicated on signage. (p. 176)

Source: Author's own table based on the Seoul Basic Plan.

5.3.   Informal planning instruments at city level

Apart from the three aforementioned formal instruments, the Seoul Building Review Standards and the Seoul POPS Provision Guideline should be considered when providing POPS in Seoul.

5.3.1.   Seoul Building Review Standard

The plans for every new building must undergo a review process arranged by planning officers. The building committee comprises experts in architecture, construction and energy, to name a few (Interviewees 3 and 4). Together, the committee members examine the appropriateness of a plan. In doing so, POPS are also reviewed according to the Seoul Building Review Standard. The Standard and the opinion of the committee members should be considered seriously if a building permit is to be obtained (Interviewees 1, 2, 4, 8 and 10).

The Standard (City of Seoul, 2018) includes a section on POPS that provides general guidance (see Table 5.6). It distinguishes five different types of POPS, i.e., pedestrian space, garden, park, plaza or piloti/sunken. Regarding planning of POPS, the Standard refers to the checklist in the Seoul POPS Provision Guideline. Aside from the type, the Standard prescribes the location of POPS, number of POPS and amenities. Among others, the emphasis is put on the location of POPS. Indeed, Interviewee 10 claims that the accessibility to (and therefore location of) POPS is regarded as the most important aspect of the review process. The Standard also states that the design of POPS may be changed to the extent that the character of the POPS is not weakened (City of Seoul, 2018).

Table 5.6 List of considerations for reviewing POPS in Seoul (Part I)

Type	POPS should be provided in the form of pedestrian space, garden, park, plaza or piloti/sunken. (Article 16 [1])
Location	POPS should be situated (Article 16 [2]): · adjacent to the main road and sidewalk to prevent private use and encourage public use; · where a minimum amount of sunshine can be obtained so that it can function as public space; · in conjunction with the street environment; · without elevation.

Table 5.6 List of considerations for reviewing POPS in Seoul (Part II)

Number	As far as possible, it should be created in one place to ensure the continuity of the resting area. (Article 16 [2] 2)
Other amenities	Pavement should maintain continuity with the pavement of the adjacent street. Amenities (e.g., planting) should be provided unless they cause inaccessibility to POPS. (Article 16 [2] 3-4)

Source: Author's own table based on the Seoul Building Review Standard.

5.3.2.   Seoul POPS Provision Guideline

The Seoul POPS Provision Guideline (City of Seoul, 2015) has three chapters: a guideline for types of POPS, a checklist for the planning of POPS, and a guideline for installing amenities in POPS.

Table 5.7 Type of POPS and its appropriate location

Pedestrian space	Pedestrian space type can be applied to an area with a high number of pedestrians or to a relatively small area. (p. 3)
Garden	Garden type can be applied to an area with a low number of pedestrians (e.g., residential area). (p. 4)
Park	Park type can be applied to an area that is bordered to a neighbourhood park or green area. (p. 5)
Plaza	Plaza type can be applied to an area with a high number of pedestrians (e.g., commercial area). (p. 6)
Piloti/ sunken	Piloti type can be applied to an area where it is difficult to secure outdoor space. Sunken type can be applied to an area that is connected to e.g., a subway station. (p. 7)

Source: Author's own table based on the Seoul POPS Provision Guideline.

The Guideline distinguishes between five different types of POPS: pedestrian space, garden, park, plaza and piloti/sunken. According to the Guideline, pedestrian space type is 'an area for pedestrians to take a short break' (City of Seoul 2015, 3). Garden type is defined as 'a cosy resting space devoted mainly to landscaping' (City of Seoul 2015, 4). Both park and plaza type of POPS are 'large-scale POPS with a size of over 500 square metres' (City of Seoul 2015, 5-6). Piloti type 'provides shelter from rain or snow, or shade in summer', while sunken type is 'an open-air space connected to, e.g., a subway station' (City of Seoul 2015, 7). The Guideline explains the characteristics of each type and

makes suggestions on where each type is appropriate (see Table 5.7) and how
to create it. Some examples are also offered to aid understanding.

Table 5.8 Checklist for planning POPS in Seoul

Accessibility	· Is it well connected with the surrounding buildings, streets and parks? · Are there any barriers to access, such as uneven street level, fencing or soundproof walls? · Is it easily accessible from surrounding streets? · Is the sidewalk separated from the vehicle road? · Is a signage installed in an easily recognisable place?
Safety/ comfort	· Is it safe from crime? · Is there lighting for use at night? · Is the safety of users considered (e.g., slip-resistant surface)? · Is inclusive design applied for the disabled and elderly? · Are facilities (e.g., AC unit, ventilation hole, machine equipment) separated from it, so that users do not feel uncomfortable?
Activity	· Can appropriate activities occur? · Is the size appropriate? · Do spatial composition and layout consider user convenience? · Is connectivity to service facilities considered?
Identity	· Is the historical and cultural environment of the area thoroughly considered? · Do materials and colour match the surrounding environment? · Does the design of amenities (e.g., bench, streetlight and artwork) match the building?
Sustainability	· Has the future development of the surrounding area been considered? · Are characteristics of place and urban environment considered? · Are materials used durable and easy to replace? · Is the design environmentally friendly and easy to maintain?

Source: Author's own table based on the Seoul POPS Provision Guideline, p. 9.

The checklist for planning POPS outlines key questions in five criteria (see
Table 5.8). This list is considered when the plans of POPS go through a review
process. Again, accessibility is a crucial issue for POPS. Aside from accessibility, POPS should also give users a sense of safety and comfort, encourage
activity. Identity of POPS and sustainability should be also considered.

Table 5.9 Guideline for installing amenities

Signage	At least one signage is required to be installed in an easily recognisable place near the entrance. Its size shall be larger than 0.5 square metres. It should be made of durable materials such as copperplate or stainless steel. Its content shall include layout, area size, amenities, hours of use and person in charge, etc. (p. 11)
Pergola	Benches are required to be installed with a roof on top. POPS may have pergola, except in spaces with a high number of pedestrians. (p. 11)
Seating	Wood materials are recommended rather than stone. Planting is required to provide shade. (p. 11)
Water features	POPS may have water features, except in main entrances or narrow spaces with a high number of pedestrians. Nozzle should be hidden. (p. 12)
Artwork	Artwork may be provided, except in spaces with a high number of pedestrians. When providing artwork, accessibility to POPS should be considered. Artwork must be in keeping with the building and its surrounding area. Artwork that gives a friendly impression may be considered. (p. 12)
Lighting	Lighting should be installed especially for use at night. (p. 12)
Paving	Paving materials should be slip-resistant and durable materials. Continuity with adjacent streets and general environment-friendliness should be considered. Pattern, material and colour of paving should match with the surrounding area. (p. 13)

Source: Author's own table based on the Seoul POPS Provision Guideline.

The Seoul POPS Provision Guideline presents guideline for installing seven different amenities on POPS in detail (see Table 5.9). To begin with, the Guideline states the minimum number of signage that should be installed in POPS as well as its location, size, material and content. Another types of amenity are the pergola and seating. Both are critical elements of POPS, as they encourage people to linger, whether it be for lunch, for a rest or to meet others. POPS may have water features or artwork to improve attractiveness and give a friendly impression, although they may not interfere with walking. Furthermore, abundant and well-designed lighting should make POPS feel safe and inviting for users 24 hours a day. Finally, the Guideline lists a number of considerations regarding paving.

5.4.   Conclusion

This research reveals that the Korean public sector was willing to engage with the private sector to provide and manage public space. As part of a process of rapid urban expansion and population growth, the Building Act was revised in 1991. As part of this revision, the relevant law for POPS was first established. Interviewees 8 and 11 explained how the two problems facing Teheran-ro – namely, the lack of walking space and resting areas, along with the high costs of public space due to increased land value – were addressed through the introduction of POPS. Concerning the former issue, Interviewee 11 mentioned that the core aim of POPS lies in securing necessary walking space and resting area; this was exactly the case in Teheran-ro. The Interviewee also claimed that even when the quality of POPS is poor at first, it can subsequently be improved. Interviewee 8 also acknowledged that land is one of the city's most important resources, but it is costly to buy land for public space in city-centre locations like Teheran-ro. Hence, the idea is to secure POPS first (i.e., in the process of development) and to make them play a role as public spaces over time.

Table 5.10 shows which planning instruments regulate which aspect of POPS. The two main categories, namely provision and management of POPS, are then divided into subcategories. Provision of POPS is regulated both at the national and city levels. With the former, since POPS are not supposed to be provided everywhere, their development first depends on the zoning dictated by the Building Act. Facility (i.e., the use of the building and its size) is also a relevant subcategory. In cases where buildings meet the conditions of zoning and facility, their owners are obliged to provide POPS. With the latter, the Seoul Ordinance on Building covers the vast majority of aspects of POPS development.

Once POPS are to be provided, further subcategories become pertinent. Interestingly, all instruments at the city level address three subcategories: location of POPS, type of POPS and amenities (other than signage). These are decisive subcategories in the promotion of POPS use. Location is important, as people are likely to be attracted when POPS are physically and visually accessible. In turn, the right type of POPS should be provided depending on the local circumstances to promote use. Significantly, indoor POPS are also regulated by one of these instruments. Although indoor POPS are not yet popular, they do have potential and may be promoted in the future. The type of POPS and the provision of amenities are related since different amenities are necessary depending on the type of POPS. Hence, instruments provide detailed information on which amenities should be provided for which types of POPS and how. These instruments are product-orientated; there is a strong focus on design to guarantee quality so that POPS can be used. Recently, signage has gained importance as it informs the public that POPS are there for them to use. This is crucial, as people would not use the space if they were unsure about their rights to do so.

Several instruments regulate the number and dimension of POPS. They also constitute important subcategories, given that POPS would not be used if they were too small. Lastly, incentivisation is an essential subcategory because good incentives can encourage building owners to provide high-quality POPS. Indeed, the fact that incentives are mentioned in the vast majority of these instruments testifies to their importance.

However, provision alone is not enough to promote the use of POPS; effective management is also crucial so that their quality as public spaces can be maintained. In fact, the policy focus has moved from provision to management since underuse or private use of POPS have been persistent problems. Management is mainly regulated at the national level. Management of POPS includes five aspects: maintenance, financial support, inspection and infraction proceedings, and use of POPS. In the case of POPS in Teheran-ro, planning instruments require building owners to take physical and financial responsibility for their day-to-day maintenance, which implies routines that make public spaces usable, clean and safe. Building owners are also required to keep amenities to desired standards. When it comes to renovation, financial support can be given from the public sector if POPS are older than five years.

In addition, the public sector conducts inspections every year to ensure that building owners comply with the law. This is crucial, as some building owners may block POPS from the public and use it for private purposes. The penalty mechanism for failing to make corrections is the core of regulation for management of POPS. When it comes to usage, the private sector regulates what can happen (or not) in POPS via rules of conduct. For the public sector, promoting the use of POPS is regarded as important, so it promotes their use through a policy that allows others to use POPS for different purposes.

Ultimately, the public sector is active in regulating both the provision and management of POPS. It is equipped with several instruments at both national and local levels. Instruments at the national level establish the legal framework; each municipality then has its own instruments consisting of legislation, guidelines and standards. Yet, while detailed legislations, guidelines and standards, may secure the minimum quality of POPS on the one hand, on the other hand, they leave little room for manoeuvre. The fact that similar or identical instruments are applied to all POPS results in only a small degree of variation.

Table 5.10 Aspects covered by planning instruments for POPS in Teheran-ro

Category	Subcategory	Direct planning instruments								
		Planning instruments at national level				Planning instruments at city level				
		Building Act (BA)	Presidential Decree of BA	National Land Planning Act (NLPA)	Presidential Decree of NLPA	Seoul Ordinance on Building	Seoul DUP Guideline	Seoul Basic Plan	Seoul Building Review Standard	Seoul POPS Provision Guideline
Provision of POPS	Zone	■								
	Facility (Building)		■			■				
	Location of POPS						■	■	■	■
	Type of POPS					■			■	■
	Number of POPS						■			
	Dimension of POPS		■			■	■			
	Signage							■	■	■
	Other amenities									
	Indoor POPS							■		
	Incentives			■						
Management of POPS	Maintenance of POPS									
	Financial support					■				
	Inspection of POPS		■			■				
	Infraction Proceedings		■			■				
	Use of POPS					■				

Source: Author's own table.

Chapter 6. Planning instruments for POPS in Mediaspree area, Berlin

Based on the case of Teheran-ro, the previous chapter elaborated how the public sector in South Korea addresses the challenge of public space provision and management by using planning instruments to promote cooperation between the public and private sectors. This chapter continues to explore the second research question, based on the case of Mediaspree area, where the public sector has exercised several instruments to engage the private sector in the provision and management of POPS (see Table 6.1). In the following sections, each of these instruments will be analysed.

Table 6.1 Planning instruments for POPS in Mediaspree area (Part I)

Indirect planning instruments	Formal planning instruments	Urban land-use planning · Preparatory land-use planning · Legally binding land-use planning
		Landscape planning · Landscape programme
	Informal planning instruments	Urban design competitions and master plans · 1992 Competition for Hauptbahnhof Berlin/Spreeufer and 1993–1994 master plans · 2000–2001 Expert review procedure of Ostgüterbahnhof · 2010–2011 Call for ideas for Kreuzberger Ufer
		Urban planning and development concepts · 1999 Area planning concept and 2001 concept for Spreeraum Friedrichshain-Kreuzberg · 2009 Kreuzberg Ufer planning concept · Urban development concept Berlin 2030

Table 6.1 Planning instruments for POPS in Mediaspree area (Part II)

Indirect planning instruments	Informal planning instruments	District development planning
		Environmental atlas
		1995 Design guideline
	Financial instruments	INTERREG II C Waterfront Urban Development
		Stadtumbau West Kreuzberg-Spreeufer
Direct planning Instruments	Formal planning instruments	Non-coverable area
		Easement
		Public easement
		Urban development contract
		Green stipulation
		Public and public authority participation

Source: Author's own table.

6.1. Formal and indirect planning instruments

As discussed in Chapter 4, Mediaspree area faces the twin challenge of securing public access to the riverside as well as public space within the neighbourhood. Rather than repurchasing properties to respond to public needs, the public sector has employed a number of planning instruments to engage the private sector. Even though POPS are still a relatively unpopular concept in Germany, the research reveals that they are increasingly found in cities where public-private cooperation is essential. A number of these POPS can already be found in Mediaspree area. This section analyses a set of formal planning instruments that indirectly affect POPS in Mediaspree area, including urban land-use planning and landscape planning. Urban land-use planning in Germany is subdivided into two categories: the preparatory land-use plans and legally binding land-use plans. Landscape planning consists of several plans; the focus here is placed on landscape programmes, which are legally defined in statute.

6.1.1.   Urban land-use planning: Preparatory land-use plan

In Germany, the major instrument of urban planning legislation is urban land-use planning.[1] The Federal Building Code states its function and the responsible party:

> The function of urban land-use planning is to prepare and control the use of land within a municipality for buildings or for other purposes, in accordance with the Federal Building Code.[2] The adoption of urban land-use plans falls within the responsibility of the relevant municipality.[3] It prepares urban land-use plans as soon as and to the extent that these are required for urban development.[4]

Since urban land-use planning forms part of a multi-level system of planning, it must be consistent.[5] Hence, urban land-use plans created by municipalities should be 'brought into line with the aims of comprehensive regional planning'.[6]

The process of urban land-use planning is divided into two-stages involving two types of plan: the preparatory land-use plan and the legally binding land-use plan.[7] To a large extent, both are governed by similar rules; however, each has a different spatial scope, scale, detail, legal form and legal effects (Pahl-Weber & Henckel, 2008). The legally binding land-use plan can only be designed on a small scale; since it does not cover the whole territory of a city, a structure plan for the entire municipal area is necessary.[8] In response, the preparatory land-use plan (hereafter FNP) outlines the type of land uses that would arise for the whole territory of a municipality in accordance with the expected urban development that will meet the municipality's anticipated demands.[9] The FNP is significant for urban development since it establishes 'the fundamental decisions of a community on how and for what purposes [...] the land available can and should be beneficially and appropriately used'

---

1   Battis/Krautzberger/Löhr, BauGB § 1 Rn. 1.
2   § 1 (1) BauGB.
3   § 2 (1) BauGB.
4   § 1 (3) BauGB.
5   Spannowsky/Uechtritz, BauGB § 1 Rn. 60.
6   § 1 (4) BauGB.
7   § 1 (2) BauGB.
8   Battis/Krautzberger/Löhr, BauGB § 5 Rn. 1.
9   § 5 (1) BauGB.

(Pahl-Weber & Henckel, 2008, 79). Its contents are described in § 5 (2) of the Federal Building Code. In particular, the FNP may emphasise the following: 'Green spaces, such as parks, allotment gardens, sports grounds, playgrounds, campsites and bathing areas, cemeteries (no. 5)'.

The above list of green spaces is by no means intended to be comprehensive. In fact, the term refers to all green spaces, whether public or private, that are 'incorporated in built-up areas and which therefore have a direct impact'.[10] The purpose of green spaces in this context is to help break up building masses, to improve microclimate or to fulfil the user needs for recreation and leisure.[11] In that sense, green spaces are differentiated from 'areas for agriculture and forest' (no. 9) as well as from 'areas for sport and play facilities' (no. 2).[12] Public bodies charged with planning tasks must adapt their planning proposals to the FNP to the extent that they have no objections to it.[13]

The FNP for Berlin is a general development plan that includes planning goals and proposals for the entire area of the city and serves as the foundation for more comprehensive planning concepts for strategic development areas and other sub-sections of the city (SenSW, n.d.-c). Out of eight different strategic planning objectives, the one that is relevant to POPS is worded as follows: 'Protection of open space, provision of recreational areas, a well-balanced urban ecology' (SenSW, n.d.-d). Berlin's FNP comprises of a zoning map and written policies. The zoning map indicates six different areas: land for building purposes, land for community facilities, land for supply and disposal plants, transport, open space and water, and areas set aside for the protection of the environment (SenSW, 2015b). Open space is then subdivided into green space (including field/meadow, park, sports ground, cemetery, water sports, allotment garden and campsite), forest and agricultural land. The written policies, meanwhile, explicitly mention public access to open space (SenSW, n.d.-e):

> To achieve the interlinking network of open spaces shown in the FNP, the legally binding land-use plans, which are drawn from the FNP, are required to establish public rights of way through sports grounds and areas of allotment gardens. Where special building areas for water sports are designated,

---

10   Battis/Krautzberger/Löhr, BauGB § 5 Rn. 20; EZBK, BauGB §5 Rn. 36.

11   EZBK, BauGB §5 Rn. 36.

12   Battis/Krautzberger/Löhr, BauGB § 5 Rn. 20.

13   § 7 BauGB.

public access, in particular to lake and riverbank, has a high priority. Public access to lakes, rivers and canals is a general long-term objective of the FNP.

Figure 6.1a FNP of Berlin, Mediaspree area, 2015

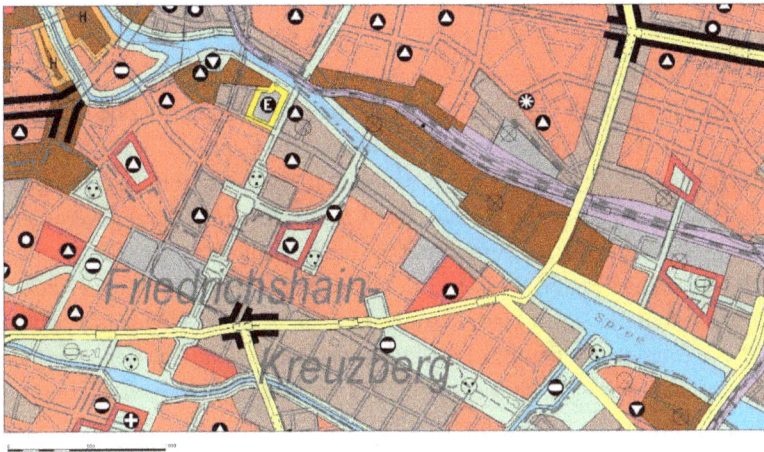

Source: SenSW, 2015c (accessed on June 18, 2018).

Figure 6.1b FNP of Berlin, Mediaspree area, 2015 (legend)

Green Areas, Water

Green area   Field or meadow
Parkland   Sports
Cemetery   Water sports
Allotments   Camping
Woodland   Agricultural land
Water

Source: SenSW, 2015c (accessed on June 18, 2018).

Figure 6.1 is part of the FNP zoning map, showing the Mediaspree area. As shown in green, the FNP requires green space on the riverside along with public access to the Spree. As the FNP is binding for the municipality, this gives justification to planning officers that they can demand POPS on the riverside.

6.1.2. Urban land-use planning: Legally binding land-use plan

The legally binding land-use plan (hereafter B-Plan) is the second stage plan, on a smaller scale than the FNP (1:500 or 1:1000 for B-Plan; 1:25.000 for FNP). The FNP serves as the foundation for the development of B-Plans.[14] In this way, the underlying representations of the FNP become more clear and concrete.[15] The B-Plan is the primary instrument for putting local government planning into action: it covers part of the municipality in terms of scale and is adopted in the form of a byelaw or municipal statute (Pahl-Weber & Henckel, 2008). It contains legally binding stipulations for urban development,[16] whose diverse contents are described in § 9 (1) of the Federal Building Code, ranging from the category and density of building and land use to areas for community amenities. The following representations are of particular importance for this research: 'Plot areas which may or may not be built on (coverable and non-coverable area)' (no. 2); 'public and private green spaces, such as parks, allotment gardens, sports grounds and playgrounds, campsites and bathing areas, cemeteries' (no. 15); 'spaces to be encumbered with public right of way' (no. 21); and 'green stipulation' (no. 25).

When it comes to new construction, nature conservation and landscape management may not always be the primary goal. Nevertheless, both must be taken into account. The establishment of green spaces can serve to offset the loss created by construction planned in the B-Plan.[17] According to no. 15, 'green spaces – such as parks, allotment gardens, sports grounds and play-grounds, campsites and bathing areas, and cemeteries – can be established in the B-Plan, at which point it should also be determined whether they are public or private green spaces'[18]. Crucially, the term "green spaces" is an um-

---

14   § 8 (2) BauGB.

15   Entscheidungen des BVerfGEs 48, 70.

16   § 8 (1) BauGB.

17   Battis/Krautzberger/Löhr, BauGB § 9 Rn. 89.

18   Battis/Krautzberger/Löhr, BauGB § 9 Rn. 82.

brella term that refers to areas that are free of solid buildings.[19] They do not have to be completely or predominantly green; the deciding factor is that their actual use corresponds to the category defined as green space in the Federal Building Code.[20] Sports grounds and playgrounds are good examples. One remarkable fact, at this point, is that non-coverable area does not belong to the category of green spaces.[21] In fact, plot area, which may or may not be built on, is also a separate element in no. 2.

The various types of private green spaces include private home gardens or riverside parks on private land. When establishing private green spaces, the interests of the property owner should be considered, as this can restrict his/her rights.[22] In addition, public right of way can be established for planning reasons both in building and non-building areas.[23] This grants the public the right to cross or use private property. In turn, green stipulation regulates matters relating to greening the area, such as designation of an area for planting trees, shrubs and any other kind of greenery, as well as the preservation of existing trees.

B-Plans in Mediaspree area have been established since the 1990s. During the era of division, the West side belonged to the "industrial area". After reunification, district officials wanted this area to become mixed-use, as supported by the newly issued FNP of Berlin. B-Plans were newly established in order to set legal framework for mixed-use area. Areas classified as open space in the FNP shall not be identified as building land in a B-Plan, except for small community facilities that serve neighbouring residential areas (SenSW, n.d.-h). As the FNP delineates green space along the riverside, B-Plans are required to secure land for green space.

6.1.3   Landscape planning: Landscape programme

Landscape planning is a planning instrument for nature conservation and land management. Its tasks include 'specifying the purpose of nature conservation and landscape management for the respective planning area and identifying applicable requirements and measures for achieving such purposes,

---

19   Battis/Krautzberger/Löhr, BauGB § 9 Rn. 82, 85.
20   Battis/Krautzberger/Löhr, BauGB § 9 Rn. 85.
21   EZBK, BauGB § 9 Rn. 126.
22   EZBK, BauGB § 9 Rn. 128a.
23   Battis/Krautzberger/Löhr, BauGB § 9 Rn. 117.

also with regard to plans and administrative procedures whose decisions may affect nature and landscape in the planning area'.[24] Plans should contain information about the requirements and measures for the implementation of the concrete goals of nature conservation and landscape management, in particular: 'For avoiding, mitigating or eliminating adverse effects on nature and landscape' (no. 4a); 'for conserving and developing recreational value of nature and landscape' (no. 4f); and 'for conserving and developing open spaces in settled and non-settled areas' (no. 4g).[25] Landscape planning thus forms the basis for the implementation of impact mitigation regulation and the improvement of both the quantity and quality of open space, especially regarding its recreational function (Böhm et al., 2016).

Landscape planning is found at several levels. In the context of POPS in Mediaspree area, the most relevant is the landscape programme (hereafter LaPro) of Berlin. The LaPro determines how Berlin wants to protect and develop nature and landscape in the city and processes the interests of the environment, nature and landscape optimally for B-Plan (SenUVK, 2017). It is binding on all authorities in Berlin whose fields of work include area development, construction projects, urban design competitions or similar tasks (SenUVK, 2017). As early as 1994, the Senate Department for Urban Development and Housing (hereafter the Senate) and the City Council had already decided to develop the riverside in Berlin as part of public green corridors of city-wide importance to be delivered through the FNP and the LaPro (Der Senat von Berlin, 2008). The LaPro and the FNP complement one another (SenSW, n.d.-f). For riverside within the city centre, emphasis is placed on making attractive areas for living and working, with public promenades for pedestrians and cyclists (Der Senat von Berlin, 2008).

Out of the four different programme plans, the programme plan for recreational use is especially relevant to this research (see Figure 6.2). Its aim is to enrich Berlin with open spaces for all, because for a growing city like Berlin, it is crucial to secure green space and a green network (SenUVK, 2017). There are two main focuses: one on the supply of open space (i.e., improving both the quantity and quality of open space), and the other on the development of an attractive green network to connect green spaces. In terms of supply of open space, empirical studies show that the maximum distance people travel daily from place of residence to green and open space is 15 minutes on foot, and the

---

24   § 9 (1) BNatSchG.

25   § 9 (3) no. 4 BNatSchG.

minimum size of green space is 0.5 hectares (SenUVK, 2017). An important method for determining deficits in the provision of open space is to compare the actual situation with the original guide value (SenStadt, 2016). According to the guidelines of Deutscher Städtetag in Berlin, 6–7 m² per person is optimal (SenStadt, 2016). In pursuit of this target, the LaPro distinguishes four priority levels for the improvement of open space supply in Berlin's residential area (SenStadt, 2016).

Figure 6.2 LaPro plan of recreational use, 2016

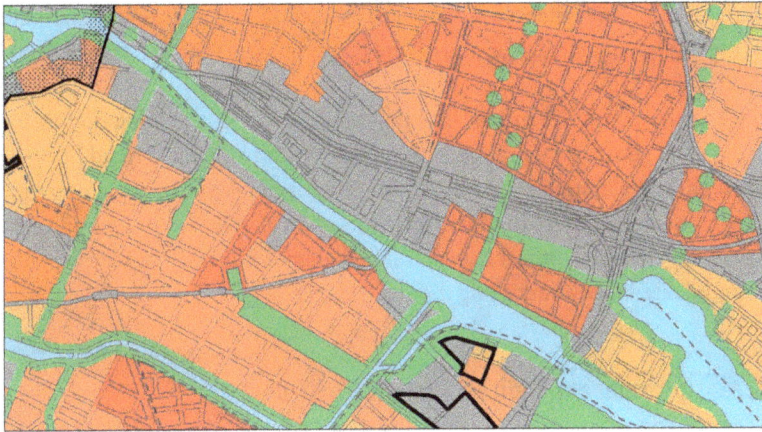

Source: SenSW, 2016 (accessed on June 18, 2018).

As shown in Figure 6.2, these priority levels are marked with four different colours. The study area is partly surrounded by the Level 1 area (in red). Level 1 is the area characterised by block development by Gründerzeit (SenStadt, 2016). As this building structure leaves little room to create or extend open space, this area is worst equipped with open space (SenStadt, 2016). Equally, demand for green space is especially high, as private or semi-public spaces are only available to a limited extent. Examples of the measures suggested for public, semi-public and private spaces in the Level 1 area include: '(a) to increase possible uses and to improve the quality of the existing open space and infrastructure areas; (b) to preserve the existing open space; (c) to connect green and open spaces; (d) to install a green courtyard, roof and façade;

and (e) to improve the quality of the street' (SenUVK, 2016b). Figure 6.2 also highlights a general lack of open space in the residential neighbourhood.

Areas marked in green in Figure 6.2 indicate green spaces and green corridors. As early as 1994, the LaPro envisaged an attractive network of walks and cycle paths to enhance the use of recreational green spaces and parkland (SenUVK, n.d.). Areas in grey are outside the residential area, including commercial and mixed-use areas, with a focus on key functions, business and services (SenStadt, 2016). The main issues here include: '(a) the development of open spaces and the potential for recreation; (b) the development of concepts for recreational use; (c) the development and qualification of small, district-related green spaces and open spaces; (d) the development of road connections; (e) protective planting adjacent to residential use and recreational use; (f) greening roof and façade; and (g) the planting of trees on suitable surfaces' (SenUVK, 2016b).

Together, both urban land-use planning and landscape planning delineate green networks along the riverside in Mediaspree area. In addition to these formal planning instruments, there are several informal planning instruments that indirectly influence the provision of POPS in the area and that justify why planning officers can and should demand open space for the public from private landowners along the riverside.

6.2.   Informal and indirect planning instruments

Several informal instruments have designated open space on the waterfront in Mediaspree area. By doing so, they have emphasised the need for both open space within the area and public access to the river itself. These informal instruments vary from master plans to design guidelines. In the following section, the most relevant instruments will be introduced and explored in relation to the provision and management of POPS in Mediaspree area.

6.2.1.   Urban design competitions and master plans

The state of Berlin recognised high development potential in the area around the former main station shortly after German reunification (SenStadt, 2001b). An **urban design competition** *Hauptbahnhof Berlin/Spreeufer* was held in 1992 for the area between Michaelbrücke and Rummelsburger Platz to restore and redefine the area (SenStadt, 2001b). The architectural firm Hemprich Tophof

Architekten won the competition with a plan that envisaged developing the area primarily for commercial use (Bezirksamt FHKR von Berlin, 2004d). Other main elements included a riverbank promenade and the creation of a riverside park, thereby exploiting the potential of the waterfront location (Bezirksamt FHKR von Berlin, 2004d). Based on this plan, the architect created a **master plan** *Hauptbahnhof/Spreeufer* in 1993. Its aim was to upgrade the surrounding area of Ostbahnhof as a location for services and offices (Bezirksamt FHKR von Berlin, 2004d).

The architect proposed a urban quarter with high density and uniform building height, while at the same time establishing a spatial relationship between the former main station and the river Spree (SenStadt, 2001b). According to the master plan, a 15-metre-wide riverside promenade would make the river on the Friedrichshain side accessible between Jannowitzbrücke and Oberbaumbrücke (SenStadt, 2001b). A park between the river and the East Side Gallery was also defined (SenStadt, 2001b). In 1994, the Senate Department of Urban Development and Environmental Protection commissioned the revision and in-depth study of the first prize of the competition from 1992 (Bezirksamt FHKR von Berlin, 2004d). In this **master plan** *Mühlenstraße*, the location of the main road was investigated, and the development of the waterfront area was discussed (Bezirksamt FHKR von Berlin, 2004d).

In 2001, Anschutz Entertainment Group (hereafter AEG), the Senate and the district of Friedrichshain-Kreuzberg carried out an **expert review procedure** *Ostgüterbahnhof* for the former East-side freight yard to develop further planning ideas for the area (SenStadt, 2003). The expert review procedure was conducted in a cooperative way as it involved several stakeholders – representatives of project developers, the Senate, the district, neighbours, owners affected and representatives of political parties in the district council – who met several times to clarify questions and formulate notes for further process (Bezirksamt FHKR von Berlin, 2005c). The jury gave recommendations for the revision of the winning plan by Hemprich Tophof Architekten, which includes Arena-Vorplatz, a public park between the East Side Gallery and the river, as well as the opening of the East-Side-Gallery for the improved connectivity to the river. A revised **master plan** was then developed based on the original plan. What is important is that the area should be developed in accordance with the objectives of the master plan and the FNP. For this purpose, the FNP was changed in parallel to allow for the development of an attractive and lively urban quarter for leisure, shopping, working and living (Bezirksamt FHKR von Berlin, 2005c). The master plan itself became part of the *Spreeraum*

Friedrichshain-Kreuzberg concept and has thus formed a planning basis for the city of Berlin (Bezirksamt FHKR von Berlin, 2005c). It also formed the basis for B-Plan V-3 (Bezirksamt FHKR von Berlin, 2005c).

As key principles for the riverside planning – such as 50 metres of minimum distance between new buildings and the riverbank – were supported in the 2008 referendum, a **call for ideas *Kreuzberg Ufer*** was launched in 2010 by the initiative *Mediaspree Versenken* for the future development of the Kreuzberg-side waterfront between Schillingbrücke and Lohmühleninsel. The focus here was on three properties in particular due to their large size: Behala, Zapf-Areal and Supermarkt (Initiativkreis Mediaspree Versenken! AG Spreeufer, 2012). Key themes included the following: 'Desires for future use – green space, housing, etc. and who builds what for whom?'.

As a model project for direct public participation, residents, experts and non-professionals were given an opportunity to develop ideas, strategies and approaches that would enable sustainable development of the riverside (Jeutner, 2011). During this 11-month period, the exhibition ran in parallel, which allowed visitors to present their ideas and comments (Jeutner, 2011). In the end, several proposals were presented and discussed, and the decision as to which proposals were recommended to the district for further development was made by three juries: a resident jury, an expert jury and voting from attendees (Jeutner, 2011). With 71% of the points awarded, the project *StadtspreeKiezspree* from the U-Lab of the Technical University of Berlin achieved the best score (Jeutner, 2011). The main idea for the project is that this area should be observed from two different perspectives: the neighbourhood and the city (Initiativkreis Mediaspree Versenken! AG Spreeufer, 2012). At the same time, the project sought to remedy the imbalance between these two levels by, for instance, linking open space along the river Spree (Initiativkreis Mediaspree Versenken! AG Spreeufer, 2012). Several solutions were developed to meet the conditions and requirements of each site, including repurposing unused barges as riverbanks (Initiativkreis Mediaspree Versenken! AG Spreeufer, 2012).

6.2.2.   Urban planning and development concepts

When making urban land-use plans, the result of urban planning and development concepts must be considered.[26] Urban land-use plans and urban

---

26   § 1 (6) no. 11 BauGB.

planning and development concepts are interconnected and indirectly affect the provision of POPS. Once adopted by a municipality, they have binding effects on public authorities. Below, three concepts are elaborated that emphasise the provision of open spaces and their connection along the river in Mediaspree area: (a) area planning concept and concept Spreeraum Friedrichshain-Kreuzberg; (b) Kreuzberg Ufer planning concept; and (c) Urban development concept Berlin 2030.

The **area planning concept** is an informal planning instrument that complements the FNP by covering a wider range of planning topics (SenSW, n.d.-g). While making the FNP, the result of the area planning concept should be considered.[27] Once the FNP is established, the concept translates the abstract policies of the FNP to their specific sub-areas – city centre, South-East Berlin, West Berlin and North-East Berlin – and demonstrates how new developments may be integrated with the existing urban fabric (SenSW, n.d.-g). The Senate first introduced the area planning concept for the city centre in 1999. The city centre is subdivided into five areas, one of which covers Mediaspree area and delineates a green corridor along the river. The relevant goals here are as follows (SenSW, n.d.-j): 'Redefinition of the riverside as public space through strengthening the riverbank; and creation of new green spaces and green networks in the immediate vicinity of the Spree'.

The *Spreeraum Friedrichshain-Kreuzberg* **concept** is a partial update of the area planning concept specifically for Mediaspree area. It was developed in 2001 via close collaboration between the district of Friedrichshain-Kreuzberg and the Senate (SenSW, n.d.-i). It represents an important basis for planning and development within the area and has a legally binding effect on all relevant stakeholders (SenStadt, 2005b). Both the district and the Senate recognised the need to open the previously inaccessible part of the riverside (Der Senat von Berlin, 2008). In response to this, the concept defines a large part of the riverside as green space, irrespective of ownership, and the desire for a several-kilometre-long promenade with viewpoints (Der Senat von Berlin, 2008). Relaxation and leisure opportunities for the adjacent densely built and underserved urban areas would also be improved through open space (Der Senat von Berlin, 2008). Indeed, the district has been successful in making the promenade publicly accessible over the course of investor development activities (Der Senat von Berlin, 2008).

---

27   § 1 (6) no. 11 BauGB.

The ***Kreuzberg Ufer* planning concept** is an update of the area planning concept and the *Spreeraum Friedrichshain-Kreuzberg* concept from 1999/2001 for the section of the Kreuzberg-side riverbank between Schillingbrücke and Köpenicker Straße 10a. An update was necessary since the view on design and planning had changed since 2001, especially as a result of the referendum of 2008 (Bezirksamt FHKR von Berlin, 2009b). In the context of this study, the applicable area includes five properties: Behala, Exil/Sage, Heeresbäckerei, Zapf and Supermarkt, which constitute plots with high development potential on the Kreuzberg-side waterfront. The basic ideas include (Bezirksamt FHKR von Berlin, 2009b) the following: 'Spatial and functional linkage of surroundings and redefinition of the riverside as public space' (2–3).

To improve this spatial and functional linkage, Spreefenster – a visual axis forming a visual bridge between the existing quarter and the river – is to be created with a width of approximately 20 metres (Bezirksamt FHKR von Berlin, 2009b). A completely closed building structure is not desired (Bezirksamt FHKR von Berlin, 2009b). Moreover, a footbridge extension of Brommystraße is planned (Bezirksamt FHKR von Berlin, 2009b). In terms of the redefinition of the riverside as public space, the district office strives for a 30-metre-wide empty strip of riverbank, 20 metres of which will be publicly accessible (Bezirksamt FHKR von Berlin, 2009b). Although the 2008 referendum confirmed that a 50-metre-wide distance between buildings and the river was desirable, this could not be met. Wherever spatial and functional linkage is not possible due to, for instance, existing buildings on the riverbank, public access will nevertheless be delivered in line with previous planning principles (Bezirksamt FHKR von Berlin, 2009b).

The **urban development concept Berlin 2030** provides city-wide development perspectives for selected urban locations in Berlin (SenSW, n.d.-k). The concept describes six qualities of Berlin as its unique selling points and sets out eight strategies for what the city is trying to achieve. Finally, 10 transformation areas are given geographical priority, providing a tangible framework to implement these strategies on the ground (SenSW, 2015a, 6). One of these strategies is called "City and green growing together". This strategy suggests that green and other open public spaces of Berlin will have been created to a very high quality and well connected and accessible to everybody by 2030(SenSW, 2015a).

Mediaspree area is located within one of the named transformation areas: Stadtspree and Neukölln. The strategy map defines public space along the riverbank. According to the concept, in 2030, Mediaspree area will be a diverse and appealing location to live which offers green spaces and recreation areas, especially along the river Spree. Plans for the Spree corridor will elicit debate; nonetheless, this area will have become a model for modern urban and spatial planning thanks to the innovative participatory procedures and "self-made-city"-style urban development (SenSW, 2015a).

6.2.3. District development planning

District development planning (hereafter BEP) is a central instrument of district planning (Bezirksamt FHKR von Berlin, 2007a). In terms of scale, it finds itself between the city-wide FNP and the parcel-sharp B-Plan. It gives shape to and, at the same time, influences the FNP (SenStadt, 2011). It aims to identify and spatially allocate the space required for different uses within a district: for social infrastructure, for green space and recreational areas, for industry, for shopping centres and retail, for public space and transport infrastructure, as well as for housing (SenStadt, 2011). BEP is binding on public authorities, and it must be considered when preparing for the B-Plan.[28]

Figure 6.3 District development planning for Friedrichshain-Kreuzberg district, utilisation plan, 2005

Source: Bezirksamt FHKR von Berlin, 2005d.

---

28   § 4 (2) AGBauGB.

The district of Friedrichshain-Kreuzberg developed its own BEP utilisation plan, published in 2005 and accompanied by a final report and
detailed plans. The report contains explanatory statements for six individual
sectors – demography and housing, social infrastructure, open space-related
recreation, nature conservation, transportation, and retail – as well as the
basis for the establishment of the utilisation plan. Regarding open space, the
final report highlights the lack of green space within the district and that the
deficit must be removed so that the district can become a liveable inner-city
location (Bezirksamt FHKR von Berlin, 2007a). Subsequently, the supply of
public playgrounds is discussed. One of the plans in detail focuses solely on
green and open space. It identifies possible locations for public playgrounds
within the district. A green network along both sides of the river is also
indicated on the BEP utilisation plan (in the form of dots). Importantly, the
utilisation plan only delineates publicly owned green and open space, which
is why a large part of the riverside is not shown in green (see Figure 6.3)
(Bezirksamt FHKR von Berlin, 2007a).

6.2.4. Environmental atlas

*Figure 6.4a Environmental atlas and its legend, availability of public, near-residen-
tial green spaces, 2016*

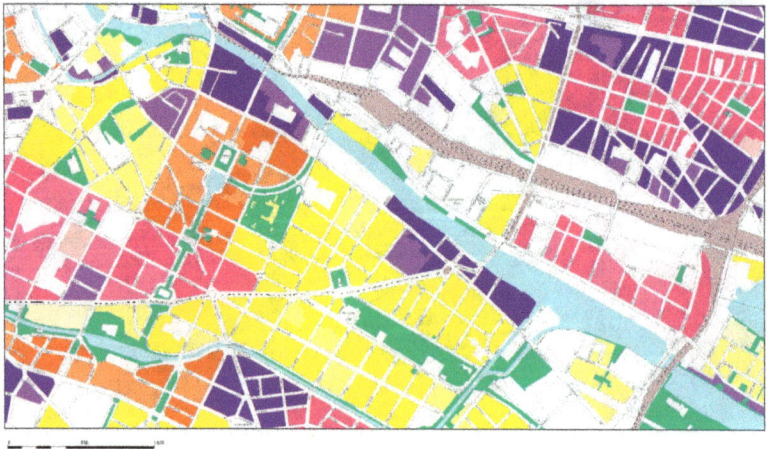

Source: SenSW, 2017 (accessed on June 18, 2018).

*Figure 6.4b Environmental atlas and its legend, accessibility
of public, near-residential green spaces, 2016*

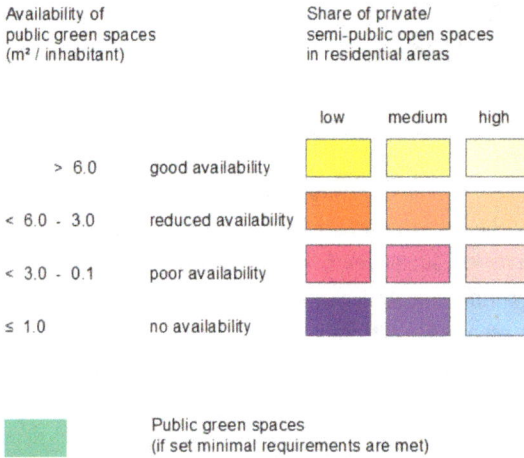

Availability of public green spaces (m² / inhabitant)		Share of private/ semi-public open spaces in residential areas		
		low	medium	high
> 6.0	good availability			
< 6.0 - 3.0	reduced availability			
< 3.0 - 0.1	poor availability			
≤ 1.0	no availability			

Public green spaces
(if set minimal requirements are met)

Source: SenSW, 2007 (accessed on June 18, 2018).

The environmental atlas is an extensive work comprising around 80 topics and hundreds of maps on the themes of water, soil, air, land use, noise, traffic, energy, climate, human and environment (SenSW, n.d.-b). It provides a comprehensive and differentiated description and assessment of the urban environment (SenSW, n.d.-b).

When it comes to the availability of public, near-residential green space, the map presents green areas, forests and residential areas with 12 different colours that are distinguished by coverage of public green space and proportion of private or semi-public open spaces. The centre of Berlin, including the area of study, is generally characterised by high building density and a small proportion of open spaces (SenSW, n.d.-a). Other than the riverside park and some green space within the residential area, the surrounding area is mostly coloured with pink and violet (see Figure 6.4). This means that less or no green space is provided and that the proportion of private or semi-public open space is very low. As a result, green space is in great need in the area, and the environmental atlas offers good evidence to planning officers to argue that the riverside should be open space for the general public (Interviewee 5).

6.2.5. Design guideline

The riverbank is understood as an important open space in the centre of Berlin and is therefore delineated in both the FNP and the LaPro as a continuous, adjoining open space. In principle, public access to the waterfront is considered essential. One study on the design of open space on the waterfront was conducted between 1995 and 2003 to establish a framework for the future development between Treptower Park and Charlottenburger Schlossbrücke (SenStadt, 2003). In the form of a design guideline, the framework provides the Senate, districts and investors with an orientation of designing building projects along the river Spree (SenStadt, 2003). The design guideline, entitled *Die Innere Stadtspree*, identifies five types of riverbank – focal point, promenade, street, connection and parkway – and describes the characteristics of each, adding recommendations for the correct type to use along different stretches of the riverbank. The most common type suggested in Mediaspree area is promenade, an example of which is given below.

The Osthafen is a former industrial port on the Friedrichshain side of the river in Mediaspree area. Publicly accessible open space on the waterfront is to be created here. The design guideline suggests a promenade version 4 – a version specifically for port areas. The guideline states that a 20-metre-wide promenade is desirable to maintain the quayside atmosphere without the need for railings (SenStadt, 2001a). The promenade should be covered by a hard covering (i.e., concrete paving) and be equipped with seating facilities and a shady spot beneath a group of trees (SenStadt, 2001a) . Lighting on the riverbank is not recommended (SenStadt, 2001a). The area should also be seamlessly connected to the existing promenade in front of the Speichergebäude (SenStadt, 2001a).

As the example above shows, the fundamental goal of the design guideline is to secure space on the riverbank and to connect open space across districts (SenStadt, 2003). On the one hand, the uniform design of the bank shall clarify the public character of the riverbank, regardless of its actual ownership; on the other hand, it shall signal its function as a superordinate route (SenStadt, 2003). This is intended to counteract the unwanted character of private space, such as a "front garden" (SenStadt, 2003).

In sum, master plans, urban planning and development concepts at both the city and the district levels, as well as the BEP, delineate a green network along the riverside in Mediaspree area. The environmental atlas underlines the existing lack of green and open space in the area, which justifies its provision. Moreover, the design guideline sets out a framework for designing the riverside for public access and use. In one way or another, then, these informal instruments indirectly influence the provision of POPS in Mediaspree area since they give justification to planning officers seeking to demand open public space from private landowners along the riverside.

6.3.   Financial and indirect instruments

Financial instruments help achieve goals; in this case, the goal is a continuous riverbank that is accessible to all. Below, two funding programmes are explored that supported several relevant measures at two different levels. They suggest that securing financial resources is one of the main concerns and that engaging private investors is inevitable.

6.3.1.   INTERREG II C – Waterfront Urban Development

INTERREG (officially European Territorial Cooperation) is a series of five programmes that began in 1989 to support transnational cooperation between regions, towns and cities within the European Union (Interreg, n.d.). In Germany, the Senate took part in EU-Programme INTERREG II C – Baltic Sea Region – Waterfront Urban Development between June 1998 and June 2001, whose common theme was the development of differently structured waterfront conversion areas (SenStadt, 2002). Out of a total project budget of €265,000, €115,000 (43.4%) were raised by the state of Berlin, and the remainder was financed through EU subsidies. As a result, a waterfront development plan for Berlin (the hereafter WEP) was drawn up in 2002.

The WEP presents the development prospects of four waterfront areas in Berlin – Spreemündung Sophienwerder, Hamburger und Lehrter Güterbahnhof, Friedrichshain-Kreuzberg, and Schöneweide – as they have favourable development chances even under changing demographic, social and economic conditions (SenStadt, 2005b). Thanks to the proximity to the historical centre and its role in joining East and West Berlin after the fall of the Berlin Wall, the Friedrichshain-Kreuzberg waterfront is given particular emphasis (SenStadt, 2005b). The guiding principle for this part of the waterfront stands for 'the sustainable transformation of a commercial and harbour district, for an innovative water-oriented urban design, for overcoming borders and barriers (the former Berlin Wall, the river and the main road), and for the coexistence of traditional and modern ways of living and working' (SenStadt, 2005a, 14). Specific measures include the following: 'Connecting individual sections of the riverbank to a network of public space; continuous riverbank, access to water and Spreebalkon as a viewpoint; development on the Kreuzberg side in harmony with the existing block structure; Lohmühleninsel as a public green area, possibly with cultural uses; and bridges to extend Manteuffelstraße and Brommystraße to interlock both sides of the banks' (SenStadt, 2005b, 28–29).

What is interesting here is that the city officials see themselves as moderators – rather than builders – who initiate and control the relevant procedures together with private actors (Der Regierende Bürgermeister Senatskanzlei, 2002). In this sense, private investment is seen to provide impetus to the waterfront conversion project in Friedrichshain-Kreuzberg, while the state of Berlin only creates the overarching framework and conditions and only supports when absolutely necessary (Der Regierende Bürgermeister Senatskanzlei, 2002).

6.3.2.   Stadtumbau West – Kreuzberg-Spreeufer

Stadtumbau West is a funding programme for urban restructuring in the former West Germany. Starting in 2004, it has financed urban restructuring measures at five different sites in the former West Berlin (Städtebauförderung, n.d.), one of which is the riverbank on the Kreuzberg side.

The area spans approximately 100 hectares over a stretch of around two kilometres of the river (Bezirksamt FHKR von Berlin, 2007b). The actual process of urban restructuring in Kreuzberg began in 2006 with a project budget of €4 million until 2010 (Städtebauförderung, n.d.). The aim of the Stadtumbau in Kreuzberg was to open, develop and urbanise the riverbank on the Kreuzberg side (Städtebauförderung, n.d.). Of the eight key aspects that define the overarching objectives for urban restructuring in this area, the following is of interest in this study: '(a) urbanising the riverside on the Kreuzberg side; (b) linking both sides of riverbank – Kreuzberg and Friedrichshain – as parts of a prosperous economic area; and (c) opening and developing the riverside for the district and city' (Bezirksamt FHKR von Berlin, 2007b, 12–13).

To achieve these objectives, numerous projects and measures – ranging from technical refurbishments to various upgrades of public space – were implemented with the support of this funding programme. As part of a step-by-step process, the focus up to 2008 was on the improvement of the living environment (Städtebauförderung, n.d.). Between 2008 and 2010, the development and opening of the underused riverside came to the fore; since 2010, the focus has been on supporting private investments, such as new construction of residential areas and the conversion of historic industrial buildings (Städtebauförderung, n.d.).

In summary, the planning instruments named in the preceding sections have indirectly influenced the provision of POPS along the riverbanks in Mediaspree area. Crucially, these instruments are interconnected and build a basis for the direct planning instruments that will be explored below.

6.4.   Formal and direct planning instruments

In the previous four sections, it was shown how various planning instruments indirectly affect POPS in Mediaspree area, shaping the decision-making environment and justifying their creation in the first place. This section will explore planning instruments that directly influence the provision and management of the four case study POPS in Mediaspree area (see Figure 7.15). In terms of type of planning instruments for POPS, the case studies include non-coverable area, easement, public easement, urban development contract, green stipulation, and public and public authority participation. All are formal planning instruments as defined in statutory provisions. Some are stipulations from the B-Plan, while others are independent instruments. Although one could argue that the B-Plan itself relates directly to sites, since not all its stipulations influence POPS, those that are directly relevant are treated as an individual instrument here.

In short, non-coverable areas, easements and public easements regulate the location of POPS, whereas urban development contracts determine who pays for the provision and maintenance of POPS and how much they pay. Green stipulation is an instrument for greening POPS. Public and public authority participation is an instrument for incorporating local opinion and knowledge around POPS into the planning process. In the following section, six regulatory planning instruments that directly influence the provision of POPS will be explored.

6.4.1. Non-coverable area

Coverable area is the area on which a building may be built. This is specified in the Federal Land Utilisation Ordinance, the most significant component in German building and planning law (Pahl-Weber & Henckel, 2008). It regulates the representation and designation of category of land use, density of land use, building method and design, and coverable area, thereby supplementing the Federal Building Code. Coverable area is determined by building line, set-back line and coverage depth, as detailed in the B-Plan.[29] Especially when it comes to a qualified B-Plan, stipulation on coverable area is essential. If a building line is established, a building must be built along this line.[30] If a set-back line is set, a building or part of a building must not extend beyond the limit.[31] Coverage depth also establishes a limit that may not be exceeded (Pahl-Weber & Henckel, 2008). Non-coverable area is any area outside the coverable area; this is where POPS can be created.

6.4.2. Easement

Easement defines which rights the landowner must grant to others.[32] Easement is regulated in the Civil Code. There are different types of easements, one of which is right of way. Right of way can be granted simply by contract between two parties – one whose land is burdened (servient land) and one whose land benefits (dominant land) – or by easement. In principle, a contract between two parties is sufficient. However, entering right of way in the land registry as easement ensures that the right remains valid regardless of changes in ownership. The owner of servient land does not always have to bear. Considerate use[33] can be demanded by the owner of servient land, if necessary. The owner of servient land can also demand a fee from the owner of the dominant land. Moreover, the owner of the dominant land is legally obliged to maintain and repair any footpaths on servient land[34].

---

29   § 23 (1) BauNVO.
30   § 23 (2) BauNVO.
31   § 23 (3) BauNVO.
32   see § 1018 BGB.
33   see § 1020 BGB.
34   see § 1021 BGB

Public right of way established in the B-Plan is another example of ease-ment if entered into the land registry. The establishment of public right of way is intended to grant the public the right to cross or use someone else's land, even against the will of the owner (Gaentzsch, 1991). Public right of way is es-tablished in the B-Plan through stipulation. The location, width and length of the footpath, as well as its beneficiary – in this case the general public – must be specified in the B-Plan (Gaentzsch, 1991). Entering public right of way in the land registry is very important since public access is then secured not only by public law (through the B-Plan) but also by private law – through easement (Interviewee 7). It is only then that the negotiated right can be transferred to the new owner in the event of sale of property. Moreover, potential purchasers can stay informed as they can always check the land registry before purchas-ing, but not necessarily the B-Plan. Since public right of way can be seen as a source of restriction, it can reduce the value of land. In cases where, from the landowner's point of view, the use of a site as determined by B-Plan solely serves public interests, then he/she has the right to claim compensation in the form of payment or transfer against payment (Peine, 1993).[35] Areas where easement is established are considered POPS since public access is secured on private land.

6.4.3.   Public easement

The most common way of agreeing public right of way is for it to be entered into the land registry. The alternative is public easement (i.e., the public-law counterpart to easement). Whereas easement is effective between landown-ers, public easement is effective between a landowner of servient land and the building supervisory authority; only the building supervisory authority can demand and enforce public easement (Peine, 1993). An owner of domi-nant land has no role in the process. If he/she wants to ensure his/her use on servient land, he/she must additionally arrange easement (Peine, 1993). In Germany, public easement is regulated via the State Building Regulation. Each state has its own Building Regulation; in the capital, it is the Building Regulation of Berlin.

Public easement is an obligation set on a piece of land. Accordingly, the landowner is required to perform, tolerate or refrain from something on

---

35   § 41 (1) BauGB

his/her land.[36] The landowner may voluntarily carry out his/her obligation to obtain an otherwise impossible building permit (Rabe et al., 2014). The contents of public easement vary and can include public easement for distance surfaces, parking spaces, playgrounds, or open space.

Public easement is not a contract between the landowner and the responsible authority. It is solely created by declaration of landowner (Rabe et al., 2014). Once it is established, it is binding on the current owner as well as any subsequent owner. This obligation remains – regardless of change in ownership – until public interest no longer exists (Rabe et al., 2014). Public easement is registered in the public easement register and can only be erased with agreement from the building supervisory authority. As public easement dictates limitations on the use of land, the encumbered land may experience a decrease in economic value, hence the need to check it before signing a purchase contract. Even though public easement is created on a voluntary basis, compensation may be demanded.[37]

6.4.4.   Urban development contract

Cooperation between municipalities and private developers has become increasingly important for a number of reasons,[38] including the shift in planning culture towards project-related planning and the need for efficient use of public funds in the provision of necessary infrastructure.[39] To correspond to this trend, the Federal Building Code regulates cooperative agreements between local authorities and private developers.

Urban development contracts are a planning instrument through which private developers are integrated into financing social and technical infrastructure. For example, the subject of an urban development contract can include 'the preparation and implementation of urban development measures by and at the expense of private developers'.[40] Land reallocation and soil decontamination are examples. Urban development contracts may also be written to promote and secure the aims pursued by urban land-use planners, in particular regarding the use of lands and the supply of housing for specific

---

36   § 84 (1) BauO Bln.
37   see § 906 (2) BGB.
38   Battis/Krautzberger/Löhr, BauGB § 11 Rn. 4.
39   Battis/Krautzberger/Löhr, BauGB § 11 Rn. 4.
40   § 11 (1) BauGB.

populations.[41] The municipality and private investors may also make an official agreement to settle the expenses or other obligations that the municipality incurs or has incurred as a result of a planned development project.[42] Regarding POPS, the municipality and the private investor can make an agreement to determine who pays for the provision and maintenance of POPS, and how much.

The Berlin model of cooperative building land development (hereafter Berlin model) has been established in the state of Berlin since 2014 to provide guidelines for the completion of uniform and transparent urban development contracts in Berlin (SenSW, n.d.-l). It stipulates that private developers may under certain circumstances assign areas for public purposes, such as public traffic areas, areas for kindergarten and primary schools, and public green space, including playgrounds (SenSW, 2018). Hence, the Berlin model provides a framework for making contracts between the local authority and private developers in providing green space in Mediaspree area.

Urban development contracts have evolved into a crucial supplementary tool in urban land-use planning and have partially replaced more traditional governmental measures like byelaws (Pahl-Weber & Henckel, 2008). In principle, the municipality acts in the interest of the public, yet this should not result in the exploitation of private developers.[43] As it may potentially conflict with different interests, a careful approach is required: 'It always has to have something to do with the project and it has to be appropriate from an economic point of view' (Interviewee 7). In most cases, a contact person will be named with whom public sector officials can jointly consider not only the use and height of the building but also where POPS should be provided, before developing a plan and entering into an urban development contract (Interviewee 7). Although this contract is not publicly accessible due to data protection, a model contract was provided by Interviewee 7:

---

41   § 11 (1) BauGB.
42   § 11 (1) BauGB.
43   Battis/Krautzberger/Löhr, BauGB § 11 Rn. 4.

Example of urban development contract regarding green space in Media-spree area (model contract)

Dedication of riverside as public green space

(1) The project is located in the planning area... in which the supply of public, near-residential green space is classified as "medium" according to Map 3 "Core Indicator Green Supply" of environmental atlas (FIS Broker, Feb. 2017, Annex 5). In a block-by-block analysis, it becomes clear that the project lies in a band of blocks between ... and ..., where the coverage of near-residential public green space is < 0.1 m² per inhabitant. This means that these blocks have insufficient public green space. According to the map "Supply of Playground – Public" (FIS Broker, Feb. 2017, Annex 5), the project is located in the planning area... whose supply level is at 4 (0.4 to less than 0.6 m² per inhabitant). This suggests that public playgrounds are undersupplied in this area. The establishment of B-Plan..., which allows further construction of housing, will make the situation even worse by causing more shortages of green space and public playgrounds.
    Based on the Landscape Programme of Berlin, Table 14 (Guide value for open and green space), 6 m² of near-residential public green space per inhabitant as well as 1 m² of public playground per inhabitant are required. For a planned floor area of ... m² for residential use,... new residents are to be expected. This leads to ... m² of near-residential public green space and ... m² of public playground. The planned public green space including playgrounds (... m²) with a total size of approximately ...m² is calculated based on this value. The project developer is aware of the needs.

(2) Berlin will dedicate the area as public green space and recreation area, which is designated as public green space in the project plan with a size of approximately ... m², pursuant to § 2 (1) no. 2 of Act on Protection, Care and Development of Public Green Space and Recreation Area – last amended on 29.09.2004. Berlin will allow cycling at walking speed in the public green area.

(3) The project developer agrees irrevocably to the dedication pursuant to (2). The approval of the project developer for the dedication is free; it is free of charge for the project developer.

Provision of public green space

(1) Berlin will create public green space, including a public playground, at its own expense. The plan is attached as an annex. Berlin will fence the riverside with a length of around 20 m from the eastern boundary of the property.

(2) The project developer reimburses Berlin for the costs of providing public green space in the amount of €... and of providing the public playground within the green space in the amount of €...

(Source: A document provided by a local planning officer)

6.4.5. Green stipulation

Green stipulation is one of the stipulations of the B-Plan, whereby certain areas may be dedicated to the planting of trees, shrubs and other kinds of planting.[44] Other kinds of planting include, for instance, grass or climbing plants for a façade or roof.[45] Green stipulation may also set out obligations relating to planting and to the preservation of existing trees, shrubs and other kinds of planting.[46] In case of the loss of greenery, replacement planting may also be obligatory.[47]

The aim of green stipulation is to make decisions specifically around greening built-up and non-built-up areas within the B-Plan.[48] Green stipulation is established for various reasons,[49] including urban design. For example, preservation of planting can reinforce a certain character for a housing development, or planting may be installed to shield or separate certain areas. Green stipulation may also be used to protect nature and landscape or to counterbalance a loss of natural environment caused by the

---

44   § 9 (1) no. 25 BauGB.
45   Battis/Krautzberger/Löhr, BauGB § 9 Rn. 150.
46   § 9 (1) no. 25 BauGB.
47   EZBK, BauGB § 9 Rn. 222.
48   EZBK, BauGB § 9 Rn. 216.
49   EZBK, BauGB § 9 Rn. 216.

construction.[50] Other reasons include rainwater infiltration and reduction of heat stress.

If a property experiences a significant drop in its value or incurs extraordinary expenditure that goes beyond the level required for the proper management of the property, the landowner is to be paid financial compensation.[51]

6.4.6. Public and public authority participation

The aim of participation is to guarantee that all possible interests are considered when making spatial plans – from state spatial planning to regional planning, urban land-use planning and sectoral planning (Pahl-Weber & Henckel, 2008). Public participation is an instrument of plan preparation, whereas public authority participation is an instrument of plan coordination.[52] In this book, public and public authority participation is understood as one of the instruments for establishing the B-Plan. Crucially, this is where local opinion and knowledge regarding POPS can be expressed. The interest level of citizens in POPS may vary depending on the location, and there may be different interests around POPS (Interviewee 7). Each interest should be taken seriously and judged fairly, which may extend the planning process. Moreover, the procedure of participation for the B-Plan is particularly rigorous, as it is prescribed by the Federal Building Code and standardised into two stages: early and formal participation (see Figure 6.5). Both the public and public authorities – including public agencies (i.e., entities to which public sector duties have been delegated by law or pursuant to a law) – are involved in this procedure.[53]

The early public participation serves to inform the public about the overall goals and objectives of the planning, as well as the alternative solutions being considered and any potential impacts of the planning.[54] It also gives the public an opportunity to discuss the planning and to give feedback.[55] Public authorities are also to be informed and are requested to state their views.[56] This phase should take place as early as possible; seeking participation of the

---

50   see § 1a (3) BauGB.

51   § 41 (2) BauGB.

52   Battis/Krautzberger/Löhr, BauGB § 4 Rn. 1.

53   Battis/Krautzberger/Löhr, BauGB § 4 Rn. 3.

54   § 3 (1) BauGB.

55   § 3 (1) BauGB.

56   § 4 (1) BauGB.

public and public authorities once a solid plan is in place does not make much sense.[57] The results of early participation are then evaluated, duly weighing public and private interests and giving fair consideration to both (Pahl-Weber & Henckel, 2008).[58] A draft plan is then prepared based on the results.

The next step, formal participation, begins with public display. Here, the draft plan, together with the explanatory statement and available comments on environmental aspects, is displayed publicly for a month.[59] Both the public and public authorities may participate prior to the deadline by making objections to the plan or by offering recommendations.[60] When giving opinions, public authorities must limit their remarks to those issues that lie within their purview.[61] In cases where the plan affects the wider area, those who express concerns should be brought into this part of the process as well.[62] Formal participation procedures for both the public and public authorities can be carried out simultaneously.[63] The results of the formal participation are evaluated, again weighing the public and private interests duly and fairly.[64] If, after formal participation, the draft plan is amended or supplemented, the formal participation should be repeated.[65] Once ready, the B-Plan can finally be adopted in the form of a byelaw or municipal statute.[66] As soon as the plan and its supporting documents (i.e., explanatory statement and summary explanation) are published, the B-Plan comes into force.[67]

In this section, six regulatory planning instruments were explored in depth to show how they are exercised to directly intervene in private property and eventually secure land for POPS. The provision and management of POPS, in turn, involves several key aspects: the location of the POPS, its financing, any necessary greening, and incorporating local opinion and knowledge. Interestingly, these instruments are used on a case-by-case basis.

---

57   Battis/Krautzberger/Löhr, BauGB § 3 Rn. 8.
58   § 1 (7) BauGB.
59   § 3 (2) BauGB.
60   § 3 (2) and § 4 (2) BauGB.
61   § 4 (2) BauGB.
62   § 4a (5) BauGB.
63   § 4a (2) BauGB.
64   § 1 (7) BauGB.
65   § 4a (3) BauGB.
66   § 10 (1) BauGB.
67   § 10 (3) BauGB.

6.5.   Conclusion

The research on Mediaspree area reveals that the public sector in Berlin was very willing to engage the private sector in providing and managing public space. In the process of the rapid privatisation and development of the Mediaspree area, issues were raised about how to secure public access to the river and to provide more public space in the neighbourhood. Rather than (re)purchasing private land, various instruments have been used to guarantee public access.

The findings based on the Mediaspree area suggest that the public sector is responsible for regulation concerning the provision and management of POPS and does so using both indirect and direct planning instruments. Indirect planning instruments shape the decision-making environment and justify the need for POPS in Mediaspree area. This is important since the public sector would otherwise be unable to require POPS from building owners. In other words, the public sector needs good reasons for demanding POPS, and indirect planning instruments help the public sector prove any deficit of space for the public within the given neighbourhood. Direct planning instruments, on the other hand, regulate POPS directly on a case-by-case basis. In fact, different instruments are used for each POPS. They are site-specific and plan-focused.

Table 6.2 shows which planning instruments regulate which aspect of POPS. There is no regulation for zoning and facility since the provision of POPS does not depend on the zone in which a building is built or its use. Instead, it depends on the local circumstances. If there is a lack of space for public use and enjoyment within a neighbourhood, the public sector would demand POPS from building owners. Subsequently, detailed arrangements would be made through the negotiation between the public sector and the respective building owner. What is interesting here is that these instruments are mainly for the provision of POPS and, to be more precise, the location of POPS. In fact, half of the direct planning instruments – non-coverable area, easement and public easement – are solely location-oriented instruments, and all the instruments except for green stipulation regulate the location of POPS. This suggests that one of the main purposes of POPS in Mediaspree area is to secure public access to the river.

The type of POPS, meanwhile, is suggested by one of the informal and indirect planning instruments, namely the design guideline. The promenade type would seem to be the most appropriate type of POPS in Mediaspree area.

Other key aspects are the number of POPS, their dimensions and their amenities, all of which can be mentioned in public and public authority participation. Yet again, this depends on the given case. In some cases, public space is a topic; in others, it is not. It is also important to note that the result of participation is not legally binding. However, it gives the possibility for people other than local planning officers and building owners to engage themselves and express their ideas and opinions. Amenities can further be regulated by urban development contracts and green stipulation. Green stipulation is an interesting instrument, as it is devoted for greening of POPS. It is regulated differently but gives detailed information, for example, on the type of planting or green roof. Other subcategories include signage and indoor POPS, but these do not seem to play any significant role. Incentives are also arranged on a case-by-case basis through urban development contracts.

Management of POPS is generally less regulated. Among five different aspects of management of POPS, the instruments examined only address maintenance and financial support. In terms of maintenance, building owners are responsible; they must ensure that POPS stay clean and safe (Interviewee 7). Conversely, there may be exceptions depending on the arrangement between the city and the building owners (Interviewee 5). Financial support to manage POPS is regulated through urban development contracts, a useful instrument in that it can cover both the provision and management of POPS. The research further reveals that there are no inspection and infraction proceedings. As Interviewee 7 notes: 'We visit POPS but we are not aware of whether they are still in line with the purpose and correspond to what was once established. But when after, for example, 20 years, you notice that there are changes and it cannot be accepted that way, then we may have to do inspections'. The question here is which department should be in charge and whether there will be enough financial and personnel resources to implement such proceedings, as claimed by Interviewee 5. Lastly, building owners themselves regulate the use of POPS through rules of conduct, while there is no instrument that explicitly promotes the use of POPS from the public sector.

In summary, the public sector is primarily active in regulating the provision of POPS, especially their location, and less active in managing POPS. Moreover, planning instruments for POPS in Mediaspree area are characterised by a case-by-case basis and a plan-focused approach.

Figure 6.5 Procedure for urban land-use planning (standard procedure)

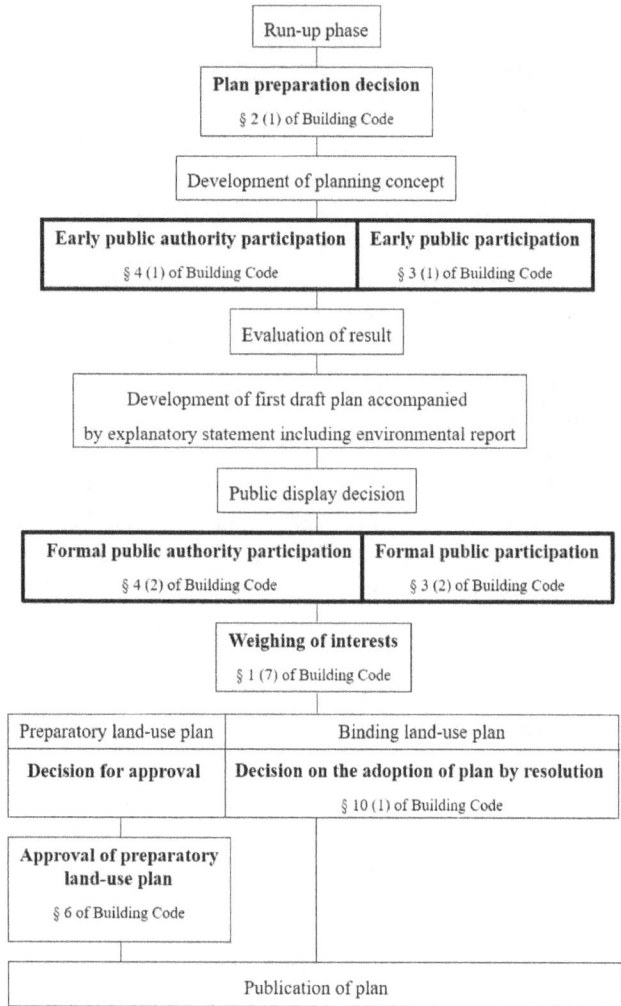

Run-up phase

Plan preparation decision
§ 2 (1) of Building Code

Development of planning concept

Early public authority participation	**Early public participation**
§ 4 (1) of Building Code	§ 3 (1) of Building Code

Evaluation of result

Development of first draft plan accompanied by explanatory statement including environmental report

Public display decision

Formal public authority participation	**Formal public participation**
§ 4 (2) of Building Code	§ 3 (2) of Building Code

Weighing of interests
§ 1 (7) of Building Code

Preparatory land-use plan	Binding land-use plan
Decision for approval	**Decision on the adoption of plan by resolution** § 10 (1) of Building Code

Approval of preparatory land-use plan
§ 6 of Building Code

Publication of plan

Source: Author's own figure.

Table 6.2 Aspects covered by planning instruments for POPS in Mediaspree area

Category	Subcategory	Indirect planning instruments			Direct planning instruments					
		Formal planning instruments (except for B-Plan)	Informal planning instruments	Financial instruments	Non-coverable area	Easement	Public easement	Urban development contract	Green stipulation	Public and public authority participation
Provision of POPS	Zone									
	Facility (Building)									
	Location of POPS	▓	▓		▓	▓				▓
	Type of POPS		▓				▓			▓
	Number of POPS									▓
	Dimension of POPS									▓
	Signage									
	Other amenities				▓				▓	▓
	Indoor POPS									
	Incentives									
Management of POPS	Maintenance of POPS							▓		
	Financial support				▓			▓		
	Inspection of POPS									
	Infraction proceedings									
	Use of POPS									

Source: Author's own table.

Chapter 7. Outcomes of planning instruments for POPS

Eight POPS in Teheran-ro and Mediaspree area were selected for site visit and analysis to better understand the planning instruments analysed in Chapters 5 and 6 and their consequences in response to the third research question: What do the outcomes of the respective planning instruments look like in reality? Four POPS in Teheran-ro and four POPS in Mediaspree area were evaluated based on the model established in Chapter 3. This model is based on a multifaceted interpretation of public space according to maintenance, accessibility and inclusiveness, each of which is measured against three discrete scales. Maintenance involves cleanliness, provision of amenities and practice of control. Practice of control means purpose of control rather than its presence. Accessibility is both about physical and visual accessibility. Lastly, inclusiveness is whether various activities can be accommodated. First, the general situation regarding POPS and the relevant planning instruments in both areas is elaborated based on expert interviews. The findings from the evaluation of the POPS are then presented, including the measurement of the three criteria based on the site visit and analysis.

7.1. Teheran-ro, Seoul

Interviews with planning officers, an architect and a building manager provided an overview of the general situation regarding POPS and the relevant planning instruments in Teheran-ro. Due to the high density of high-rise buildings in the area, there is also a high proliferation of POPS. These spaces are provided by building owners in accordance with legislation, guidelines and standards produced by the public sector at two different levels; planning instruments at the city level are in line with those at the national level. Building line in Teheran-ro is defined by DUP, which means buildings should be in contact with the designated building line (Interviewee 10). Consequently, POPS are created at the corner, as a piloti type or behind the adjacent building. The Interviewee from the district's planning office expressed concern that building owners were providing POPS for their own benefits rather than for the general public. What is more, some building owners are hesitant to open POPS 24/7 due to the amount of maintenance work incurred, which leads to conflict between building owners and users. A building manager of one of the buildings in Teheran-ro also mentioned conflicts among users – between smokers and non-smokers, for instance.

Nevertheless, public interest in POPS in the district is generally low since POPS are not always provided, and their size varies hugely (Interviewee 1). Complaints are occasionally submitted to the district when the use of POPS is prohibited (Interviewee 1). Although a database of POPS is available from the Ministry of Land, Infrastructure and Transport, where citizens can inform themselves about and leave comments regarding POPS, this interaction is rare: 'Citizens do not seem to know about the existence of the database. Also, it does not really have any functions except for leaving comments' (Interviewee 8).

POPS in Teheran-ro tend to be used passively; they are often used by office workers for smoking (Interviewee 1). They are busy, especially during lunchtime (Interviewee 16). Until the summer of 2017, no applications were submitted for the use of POPS: 'From the building owners' perspective, it will not be easy to lend their POPS to "strangers". But, in case of cultural events, building owners might approve as they can also benefit from the publicity effect' (Interviewee 1).

One interviewee, who is a district planning officer, highlighted the private use of POPS as well as the absence of signage as the most common violations of regulations. Private use includes the selling of goods by the owner or tenant of a building (Interviewee 8). Although penalties are imposed whenever building owners fail to make corrections within a given period, Interviewees 3 and 8 questioned their effectiveness of penalty because the process of imposing the fine takes months. As a result, some building owners can violate the law and then correct the fault when they are caught before having to pay a penalty. They can also exploit loopholes in the law and simply repeat the malpractice. Hence, these interviewees argued that fines should be imposed immediately. Similarly, although inspections should be conducted once every year, this proves challenging due to the sheer number of POPS (Interviewee 1).

Many of the POPS in Teheran-ro were provided between the 1990s and the 2010s. Planning instruments get updated over time, hence there are changes. Although older legislations, guidelines and standards were applied at the time, these POPS still need to comply with current regulations and standards to some extent. Examples of this include the requirement to install at least one signage at the entrance of the POPS or the use of POPS for a maximum of 60 days in a year. Both apply to all POPS, no matter which regulations were applied previously. Four POPS in Teheran-ro that were created from 1999 to 2010 were selected and evaluated. These POPS show how the planning instruments are exercised in practice. Lastly, the results of the evaluation of the POPS are presented based on the site visit and analysis.

Figure 7.1 Photo of Teheran-ro

Source: Author's own photo.

Figure 7.2 Location of four selected POPS in Teheran-ro

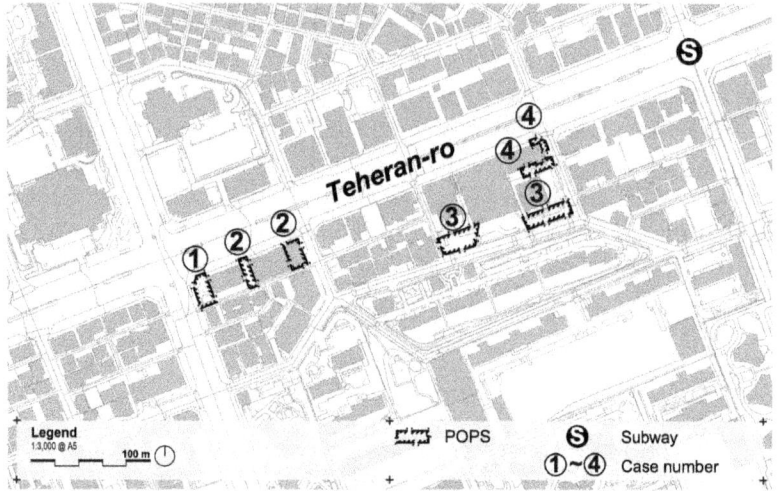

Source: Author's own figure.

7.1.1.   POPS Case 1: Teheran-ro 302

POPS Case 1 is located at an intersection of two main roads: Teheran-ro and Eonju-ro. As a result, there is a high pedestrian flow on the adjoining sidewalks. POPS Case 1 was visited several times in June 2017 – on weekdays and on weekends, between 7 a.m. and 11 p.m. – to analyse and evaluate it based on maintenance, accessibility and inclusiveness.

This POPS is well maintained in the sense that it is usable, clean and safe. It provides a litter receptacle and has no fly tipping or fly posting. Its amenities are kept to desired standards. Aside from the litter receptacle, it provides basic amenities such as pergola and bench, and a piece of artwork stands at its centre. This artwork seems to be relatively large for the size of POPS; however, according to the observation, many people use the lower part as a seat. A drinking fountain is installed, but this is blocked from use. Signage is installed at one of the entrances. Although it does not include information like area size, list of amenities, hours of use or person in charge (as suggested by the Seoul POPS Provision Guideline), it does indicate that the space is for citizens to use. Lighting is lacking; however, the area remains bright until 10p.m.

due to light from the adjoining Dunkin Donuts outlet. Regarding practice of control, a sign indicates "cigarette butts in the litter receptacle"; this is the only rule on behaviour. This does not reduce the publicness of the POPS, as it tries to exclude anti-social behaviours only. In sum, three points are given to each indicator for the dimension of maintenance.

In terms of physical accessibility, parts of the POPS front onto sloping streets and are hence accessible via stairs. Another entrance is at the same level as the adjoining sidewalk with barrier-free pavement and good connection to the adjacent street. The POPS is a plaza of the sunken type and is surrounded by a wall that makes it less visible from the sidewalk while providing a sense of cosiness for those who use the space (although this is purely due to topography). Hence, three points are given to each indicator for the dimension of accessibility.

Inclusiveness depends on the other two criteria as well as the size of the POPS. Currently, this POPS can accommodate activities like sitting, taking a break, smoking and having a conversation. Due to its size, it is unlikely that any other uses can be accommodated. Yet, thanks to its provision of amenities, less control and high accessibility, it has the potential to be used by all regardless of gender, age, race or disability. From my observations, this POPS is mostly used by office workers from the building. However, this is not necessarily due to the design of the POPS, but rather because it is surrounded mainly by office and commercial units. Given that the main users are office workers, the POPS is busy during lunchtime on working days, but less used during the night or on weekends. This POPS is an open space, meaning it may be used less during the winter or the rainy season. In sum, two points are given for the dimension of inclusiveness.

Figure 7.3 Evaluation of POPS Case 1

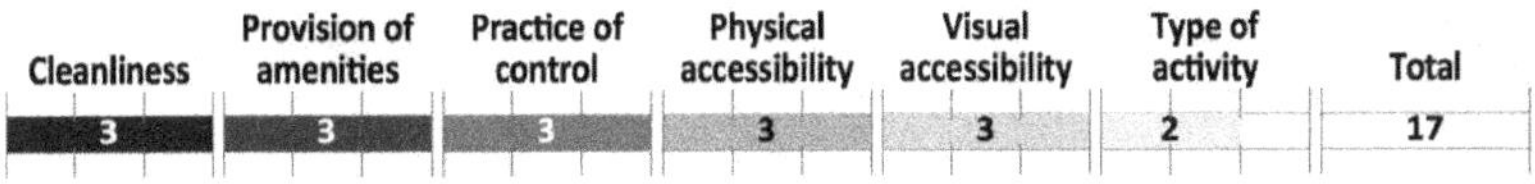

Cleanliness	Provision of amenities	Practice of control	Physical accessibility	Visual accessibility	Type of activity	Total
3	3	3	3	3	2	17

Source: Author's own figure.

Table 7.1 Information for POPS Case 1

Address	Teheran-ro 302
Building use	(Mainly) office use
POPS type	Plaza/sunken
POPS size	-
Amenities	Pergola, bench, planting, litter receptacle, artwork, drinking foun-tain (out of use), signage

Source: Author's own table.

Figure 7.4 POPS Case 1 site map

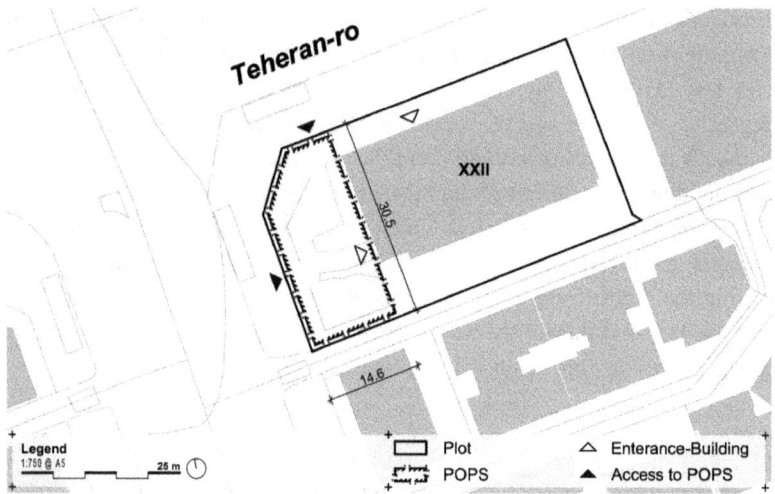

Source: Author's own figure.

Figure 7.5a Photographs for POPS Case 1: POPS during the day

Source: Author's own photo.

Figure 7.5b, c Photographs for POPS Case 1: POPS during the night and entrance to POPS

Source: Author's own photos.

Figure 7.5d, e Photographs for POPS Case 1: Drinking fountain blocked from use and signage indicating POPS

Source: Author's own photos.

7.1.2.   POPS Case 2: Teheran-ro 306

POPS Case 2 is divided into two spaces and is located at two corners of the building. One of them has a piloti structure and thus has a roof, while the other is an open space. POPS Case 2 was visited several times in June 2017 – on weekdays and on weekends, between 7 a.m. and 11 p.m. – to analyse and evaluate it based on maintenance, accessibility and inclusiveness.

Regarding maintenance, both POPS are usable, clean and safe. They have no fly tipping or posting. Yet, they provide fewer amenities than Case 1. The POPS with the piloti structure does not provide any amenities except for lighting and a signage; it does not even contain seats. The other POPS provides seating and planting but does not have any signage. Interestingly, neither POPS provides litter receptacles. In both POPS, signs indicate that they are smoking-free areas. This does not reduce the publicness of either POPS, as they are attempting to exclude anti-social behaviours only. Hence, three points are given for cleanliness and practice of control; two points are given for provision of amenities.

In terms of accessibility, both POPS are easily accessible from Teheran-ro and are barrier-free. The one with the piloti structure is situated in front of one of the entrances to the building, where there is a constant flow of people. Thus, three points are given for both physical and visual accessibility.

Inclusiveness depends on the other two criteria as well as the size of the POPS. For inclusiveness, the piloti POPS may be used by pedestrians to take brief shelter from the rain. Due to the lack of amenities and size, it is unlikely that this POPS could accommodate other uses. Use of this POPS may not be desired in any case since it is located directly in front of the entrance and can disturb human traffic. The other POPS may be used for sitting and taking a break, especially in summer, thanks to the shade provided by planting. However, large ventilation holes seem to discourage its use. What is more, since this POPS is a no-smoking area, it is less used by office workers. Rather, according to the observation, the space is used for passing through to the next street and has the sense of a leftover space between two high-rises. The absence of lighting also means it is unused at night. As it is an open space, it may be even less used during the winter or rainy season. Hence, one point is given for the dimension of inclusiveness.

Figure 7.6 Evaluation of POPS Case 2

Cleanliness	Provision of amenities	Practice of control	Physical accessibility	Visual accessibility	Type of activity	Total
3	2	3	3	3	1	15

Source: Author's own figure.

Table 7.2 Information for POPS Case 2

Address	Teheran-ro 306
Building use	Office use, others
POPS type	Piloti/plaza
POPS size	202.3 m^2
Amenities	Bench, lighting, planting, signage

Source: Author's own photos.

Figure 7.7 POPS Case 2 site map

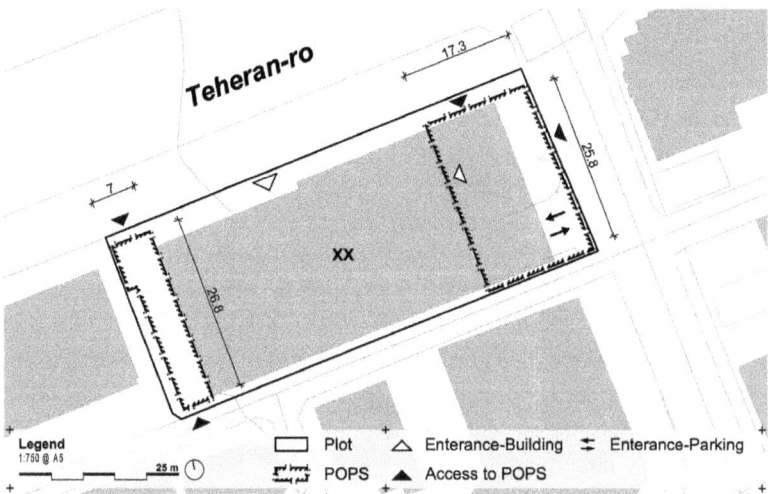

Source: Author's own figure.

Figure 7.8a Photographs for POPS Case 2: POPS with piloti structure

Source: Author's own photo.

Figure 7.8b, c Photographs for POPS Case 2: Entrance to POPS with piloti structure and second corner POPS

Source: Author's own photos.

Figure 7.8d, e Photographs for POPS Case 2: Ventilation holes next to POPS and signage indicating POPS

Source: Author's own photos.

7.1.3.   POPS Case 3: Teheran-ro 322

POPS Case 3 is divided into two spaces. Unlike Cases 1 and 2, neither POPS adjoins Teheran-ro; they are situated behind the building, although both are connected to one of the entrances. POPS Case 3 was several times in June 2017 – on weekdays and on weekends, between 7 a.m. and 11 p.m. – to analyse and evaluate it based on maintenance, accessibility and inclusiveness.

In terms of maintenance, both POPS give the impression that they are well cared for. Both are usable, clean and safe. They have no fly tipping or posting, and their amenities are kept to desired standards. The POPS provide amenities like benches, planting, artwork and lighting. Following a conflict between smokers and non-smokers, a smoking area was designated in one of the POPS (Interviewee 16). Smoking is forbidden outside this designated area. Apart from smoking, the POPS are used for rest; indeed, one of the POPS has many trees providing comfort, shade and textural variety. Signage is provided in both POPS. Although the signage does not include information like area size, amenities, hours of use or person in charge (as suggested by the Seoul POPS Provision Guideline), it still indicates that these spaces are for citizens to use. Signs also indicate that the POPS are smoking-free areas except for the designated smoking area. This may not reduce publicness, as it tries to exclude anti-social behaviours only. However, other signs that indicate the use of camera surveillance 24/7 may give the sense of control. Hence, three points are given for cleanliness and provision of amenities; two points are given for practice of control.

In terms of accessibility, both POPS are free of physical or visual barriers. Both are located behind the building, meaning they are accessible not directly from Teheran-ro but from a side street. While there are fewer pedestrians, both POPS abut onto a residential area and so are potentially used by residents. Hence, three points are given for physical and visual accessibility.

For inclusiveness, both POPS are mainly used for taking a rest, smoking or having a conversation. Interviewee 16 was sceptical about other uses, not only due to the design of the POPS but also due to multiple ownership: 'It is generally difficult to meet an agreement'. Nevertheless, according to the observation, POPS Case 3 was the most actively used POPS with a wide range of groups of people: not only office workers but also residents, the elderly, and so on, possibly due to the adjoining residential area. Another reason may be the division of use: while one POPS is mainly used by smokers as it has a designated area for smoking, the other is a smoke-free area and has a different character with more benches and planting. Interviewee 16 admitted that this minor intervention has created less conflict between smokers and non-smokers. The fact that both POPS are clean, provide amenities and are adequately accessible could be another contributing factor. As there is lighting (though not everywhere), both areas are used at night as well. Although use may be dependent on weather and season, three points are nonetheless given for the dimension of inclusiveness.

Figure 7.9 Evaluation of POPS Case 3

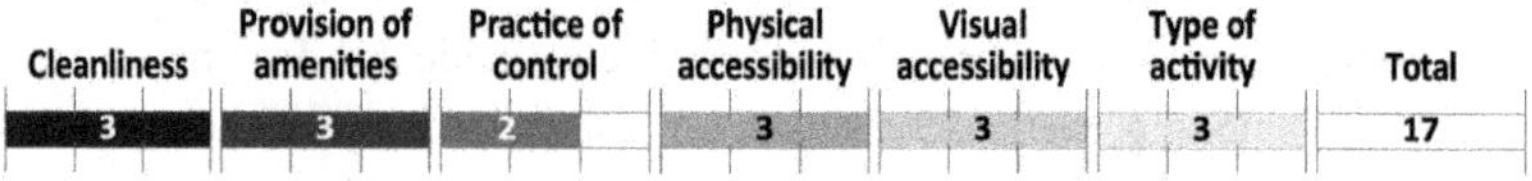

Cleanliness	Provision of amenities	Practice of control	Physical accessibility	Visual accessibility	Type of activity	Total
3	3	2	3	3	3	17

Source: Author's own figure.

Table 7.3 Information for POPS Case 3

Address	Teheran-ro 322
Building use	Office use, others
POPS type	Garden
POPS size	500 m²
Amenities	Pergola, bench, lighting, planting, smoking facility, signage

Source: Author's own table.

Figure 7.10 POPS Case 3 site map

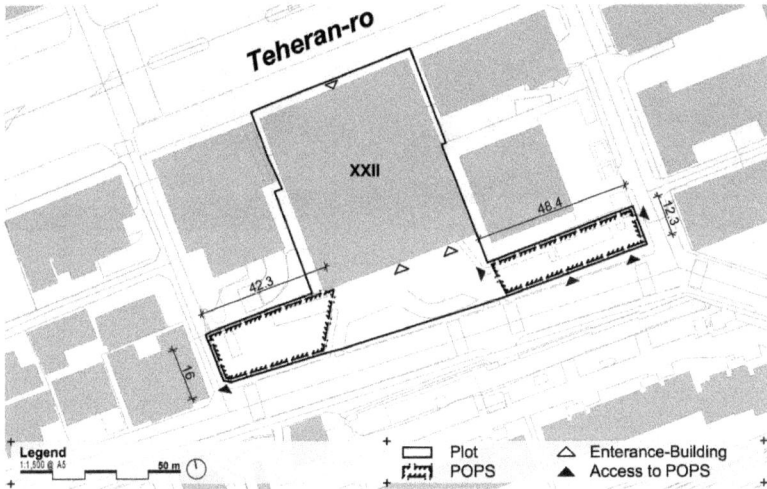

Source: Author's own figure.

Figure 7.11a Photographs for POPS Case 3: POPS with resting area

Source: Author's own photo.

Figure 7.11b,c Photographs for POPS Case 3: POPS with resting area and designated smoking area

Source: Author's own photos.

Figure 7.11d,e Photographs for POPS Case 3: Signage indicating POPS and sign indicating the presence of surveillance camera

Source: Author's own photos.

7.1.4.   POPS Case 4: Teheran-ro 326

POPS Case 4 is also divided into two spaces. One is located in front of the building and adjoins Teheran-ro; the other is behind the building. POPS Case 4 was visited several times in June 2017 – on weekdays and on weekends between 7 a.m. and 11 p.m. – to analyse and evaluate it based on maintenance, accessibility and inclusiveness.

In terms of maintenance, both POPS are usable, clean and safe. They have no fly tipping or posting. The amenities are kept to desired standards. However, a marked difference was observed in the provision of amenities between the two POPS. While the one situated in front of the building offers no amenities, except for a signage, the other POPS offers benches, planting, shelter and a litter receptacle so that office workers – the main users of the space – can take a rest. Both POPS have signage, yet this does not include information about amenities or the person in charge (as suggested by Seoul POPS Provision Guideline). Regarding practice of control, the POPS in front of the building has a sign indicating it is a smoking-free area. This may not reduce publicness, as it tries to exclude anti-social behaviours only. On the other hand, other signs indicating the use of camera surveillance 24/7 may give the sense of control. The POPS behind the building includes a sign delineating smoking and non-smoking areas, and another indicating that rubbish should be thrown in the litter receptacle. To sum up, three points are given for cleanliness, and two points are given for provision of amenities as well as practice of control.

For accessibility, the POPS in front of the building is connected to the sidewalk on Teheran-ro, meaning it is both physically and visually accessible. It is of the pedestrian space type, while the other POPS is a plaza behind the building that is almost invisible due to its narrow entrance. The gate is open between 7 a.m. and 7 p.m. only. During the night, access is only possible through the lobby where there is a security guard. Hence, two points are given for physical and visual accessibility.

For inclusiveness, the POPS in front of the building is simply too small and narrow to accommodate any use. It provides no amenities apart from a signage. In fact, according to the observation, it is less used regardless of time or weather. The POPS behind the building, meanwhile, is mainly used by office workers from the building for taking a rest and smoking. It is especially busy during lunchtime on working days. Although it is clean and provides amenities, due to its location and lower visibility, it does not have the potential to be used by other groups beyond the office workers. As a result, this POPS may be less used during the night or on weekends. Hence, one point is given for inclusiveness.

Figure 7.12 Evaluation of POPS Case 4

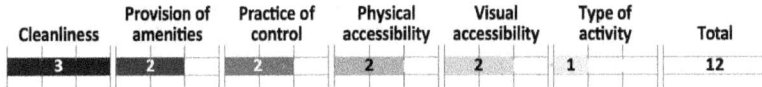

Cleanliness	Provision of amenities	Practice of control	Physical accessibility	Visual accessibility	Type of activity	Total
3	2	2	2	2	1	12

Source: Author's own figure.

Table 7.4 Information for POPS Case 4

Address	Teheran-ro 326
Building use	Office use
POPS type	Plaza/pedestrian space
POPS size	110.86 m²
Amenities	Pergola, bench, lighting, planting, litter receptacle

Source: Author's own table.

Figure 7.13 POPS Case 4 site map

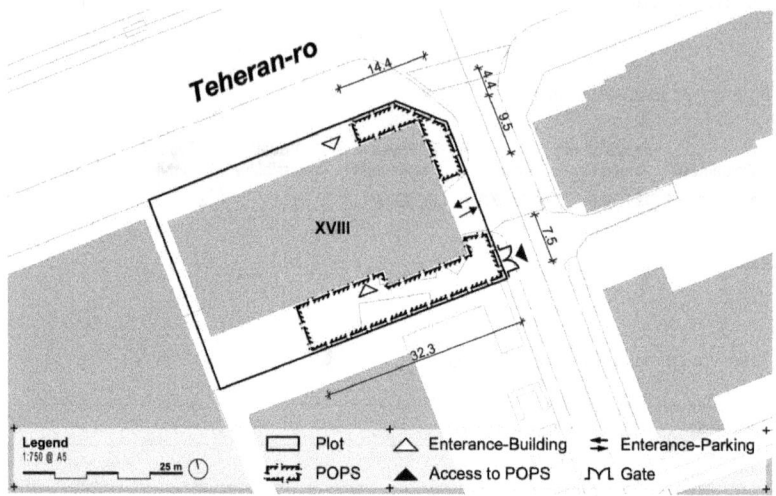

Source: Author's own figure.

Figure 7.14a Photographs for POPS Case 4: Hidden POPS behind the building

Source: Author's own photo.

Figure 7.14b, c Photographs for POPS Case 4: Sign indicating smoking and non-smoking areas and closed gate to POPS

Source: Author's own photos.

Figure 7.14d, e Photographs for POPS Case 4: Signage indicating POPS and POPS adjoining sidewalk in Teheran-ro

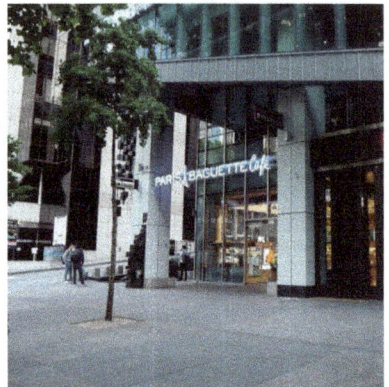

Source: Author's own photos.

7.2.   Mediaspree area, Berlin

Interviews with planning officers in Friedrichshain-Kreuzberg gave an overview of the general situation regarding POPS and the relevant planning instruments in Mediaspree area. First, they revealed a level of high demand for open space within the district. In Kreuzberg, green spaces are largely developed, and there is not much space remaining for creating new green spaces. Nonetheless, district officials want to create public green space along the river Spree so that the whole course of the river can be experienced by citizens (Interviewee 5). This Interviewee pointed to two options to realise this objective:

> First, we as the public sector buy a piece of land along the river, but it is seldom the case because we do not have the resources. Second, through several instruments, we demand that building owners provide POPS in the form of green space. Therefore, it is important to prove that the neighbourhood has a deficit of green space. Otherwise, the law does not allow us to require that from owners. We are only allowed to demand it when we have well-established reasons.

Interviewee 5 named the instruments that give the district justification to require POPS. First, the F-Plan clearly delineates a path on the riverbank. Second, the riverside on the Kreuzberg side is subject to old planning law that needs to be updated by establishing the B-Plan. The environmental atlas also presents evidence of the need for more green space within the district, as do other urban concepts. Above all, the result of 2008 referendum offers numerous reasons for requiring POPS, and although the district cannot implement them to a full extent, it has been trying to adopt them (Interviewee 5). Evidently, the district is in negotiation with private investors:

> We do not need to buy it. The owner keeps ownership and has certain rights as the owner. Nevertheless, it is a public green area. This is a normal procedure. Of course, we sometimes have projects where we cannot come to an agreement and have to force the owner. But investors know that there is no point (Interviewee 5).

Both Interviewees 5 and 6 named POPS-related instruments that are exercised on the riverside within the district.

Four POPS in Mediaspree area were selected and evaluated. These POPS show how the six planning instruments that directly influence POPS in Mediaspree area are used in practice. B-plans have been established in all cases. Hence, thanks to the explanatory statements of B-Plan, it was possible to ascertain which instruments had been exercised where and their contents in detail. Lastly, the results of the evaluation of the POPS are presented based on the site visit and analysis.

Figure 7.15a Locations and planning instruments for four selected POPS in Mediaspree area

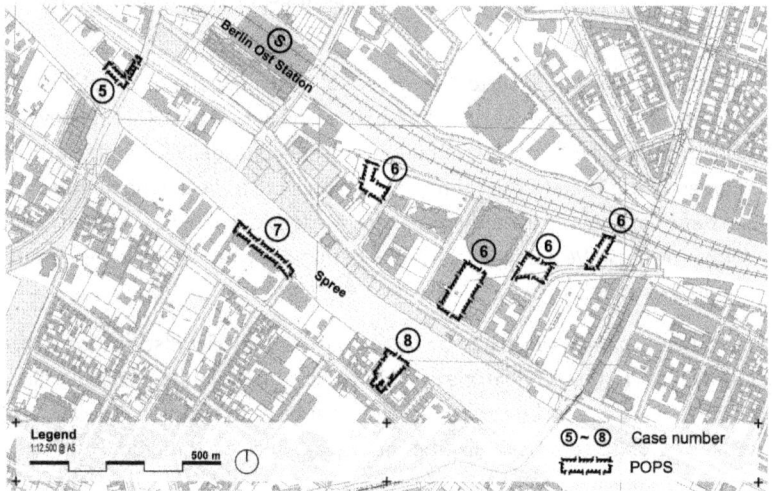

Figure 7.15b POPS Case 5: Holzmarktstr. 34

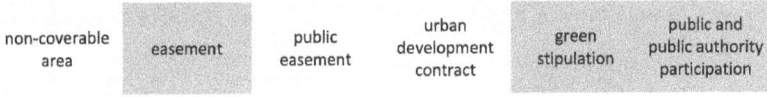

non-coverable area	easement	public easement	urban development contract	green stipulation	public and public authority participation

Figure 7.15c POPS Case 6: Mercedes-Benz Arena

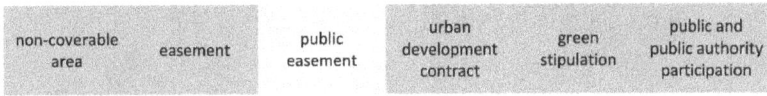

non-coverable area	easement	public easement	urban development contract	green stipulation	public and public authority participation

Figure 7.15d POPS Case 7: Köpenicker Str. 16-17

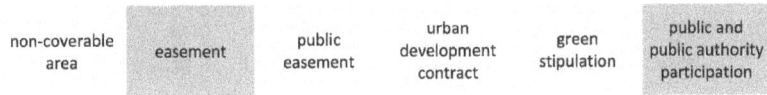

non-coverable area	easement	public easement	urban development contract	green stipulation	public and public authority participation

Figure 7.15e POPS Case 8: Pfuelstr./Köpenicker Str.

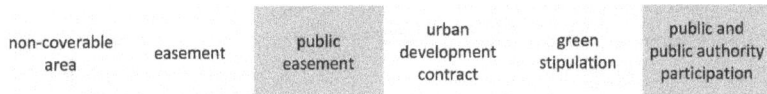

non-coverable area	easement	public easement	urban development contract	green stipulation	public and public authority participation

Source: Author's own figures.

7.2.1.   POPS Case 5: Holzmarktstr. 34

Figure 7.16 Stipulations in graphic form regarding easement at POPS Case 5

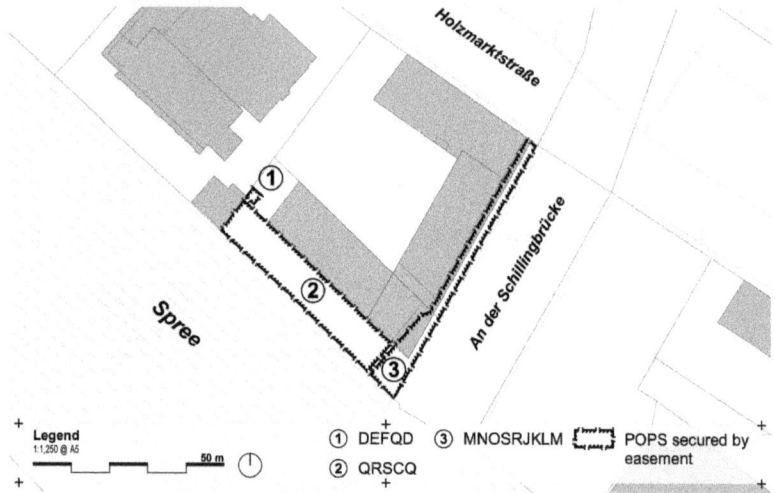

Source: Author's own figure based on B-Plan V-61.

Stipulations in textual form regarding easement at POPS Case 5

- **No. 11:** Public right of way is set for the area MNOSRJKLM and DEFQD.
- **No. 14:** Public right of way is set for the area QRSCQ along the river Spree with a width of at least 3.5 m (revised on Sep. 25, 2000).

(Source: B-Plan V-61)

This section involves an analysis of B-Plan V-61 and its explanatory statement.[1] The site comprises of 3,962 square metres and is situated north of the river Spree, on the Friedrichshain side. The property is privately owned, having

---

1   See Bezirksamt FHKR von Berlin, 2000a, 2000b.

been sold to an investor in 1997 during the second bidding procedure. To-day, the building is used for apartments, offices, a hotel and retail stores and restaurants. Three instruments are exercised here in terms of POPS: ease-ment, green stipulation, and public and public authority participation.

As illustrated in Figure 7.16, public right of way is established on the river-side (see written stipulation no. 14) to make the area publicly accessible. Pub-lic right of way is also established along the street An der Schillingbrücke (see written stipulation no. 11) to offer space for pedestrians, as well as at the north-west border of the area for the possible continuation of the promenade with neighbouring property in the future (see written stipulation no. 11). Pub-lic right of way is supposed to be entered accordingly in the land registry as easement.

Figure 7.17 Stipulations in graphic form regarding green stipulation at POPS Case 5

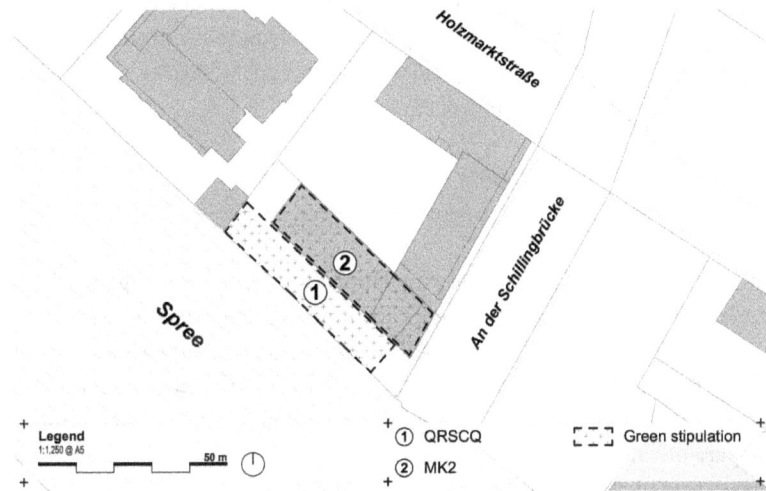

Source: Author's own figure based on B-Plan V-61.

Stipulations in textual form regarding green stipulation at POPS Case 5

· **No. 8:** The area QRSCQ is to be planted in a way that creates the impression of a riverside promenade. Plantings are to be preserved.
· **Recommendation:** When applying this written stipulation, it is recommended to use the following list of plants. Tree species – Salix alba, Acer platanoides, Tilia cordata and Quercus robur. Shrub species – Cornus mas, Corylus avellana, Euonymus europaeus, Prunus padus and Rhamnus frangula.
· **No. 9:** The areas for planting are to be designed horticulturally and maintained. Plantings are to be preserved. This also applies when underground garages are provided under these areas. [...] The obligation for planting does not apply to paths and squares.
· **Recommendation:** When applying this written stipulation, it is recommended to use the list of plants attached to written stipulation no.8.
· **No. 10:** In the core area MK2, flat roofs of buildings with an area of more than 200 m² are to be greened; this does not apply to technical facilities or to lighting surfaces or roof terraces.

(Source: Explanatory statement V-61, pp. 22-23)

In addition to easement, green stipulation is exercised (see Figure 7.17). A green ordinance sets arrangements for greening the riverside path, open space and flat roofs. The continuation and design of promenade along the river Spree is a key goal of the B-Plan V-61. It sets out the legal framework for greening the riverside path (see written stipulation no. 8). The riverside area, as part of the long promenade, shall 'characterise the Friedrichshain-side waterfront in a uniform design and contributes to the visual identity of the waterfront' (Bezirksamt FHKR von Berlin, 2000b). According to the design guidelines by GuD Geotechnik und Dynamik Consult GmbH, a double row of trees is envisaged to divide spaces between building, paths and the riverside. When planting, plant species that correspond to the local flora, and which respect the site condition, are to be chosen. As a recommendation, a list of tree and shrub species taken from the design guidelines and landscape planning related expert contribution is provided. The green ordinance outlines the requirements for greening and the preservation of the pervious open space (see written stipulation no. 9). This is 'the result of the impact balance and is justified by the imperviousness within the area as well as the prevailing lack of open space in the surrounding area'(Bezirksamt FHKR von Berlin, 2000b). The use of open space within the block is significant given the low possibility of creating green and open space. The area may be upgraded and the shortage of open space can be minimised by restricting imperviousness and implementing intensive greening measures. As an ecological measure, greening roofs is becoming increasingly important. Hence, it is established in a part of the area (see written stipulation no. 10).

Furthermore, public and public authority participation plays an important role here. One of the significant contributions of B-Plan V-61 to the well-being of the general public is the publicly accessible riverside path. Public and public authority participation took place in the form of early and formal participation. During the public display, three suggestions were made by a department named Fachabteilung Abt. Bau-Wohn Stadtp L1 regarding POPS, namely the list of tree and shrub species (see box below). Suggestions were evaluated but did not lead to an amendment of the plan.

Suggestions made during the formal public authority participation and results of weighing relevant to POPS Case 5

- **Suggestion 1:** Concerning the recommendation of written stipulation no. 8 – the two tree species listed in the recommended planting list are not complete.
- **Weighing 1:** Four tree species are listed as recommendations. Since the complete list contains over 40 tree species, only the most suitable tree species are listed here. As this is merely a recommendation, it is not restricted to these four species.
- **Suggestion 2:** The shrubs listed as recommendations are not suitable for the riverside promenade.
- **Weighing 2:** It is true that, according to the written stipulation no. 9, the riverside promenade should be planted with trees only. The list is, however, not only for the riverside, which is why it includes both tree and shrub species.
- **Suggestion 3:** The euonymus europaeus listed as a recommendation is considered dangerous and should not be recommended.

> ·   **Weighing 3:** Euonymus europaeus is an important habitat for several
>   birds. It cannot be required that all open spaces must avoid euonymus eu-
>   ropaeus; this would be undesirable for ecological reasons.
>
> *(Source: Explanatory statement V-61, pp. 29-30)*

POPS Case 5 was visited three times during the day in November 2017 as well
as in May and July 2018. The site analysis reveals that all three POPS are well
cared for; they are usable, clean and safe. They have no fly tipping or posting, and the amenities are kept to desired standards. In terms of amenities,
benches, planting, lighting and litter receptacle are provided in the POPS at
riverside, and trees create the impression of a riverside promenade. The other
two POPS do not offer any amenities; given the lack of space, they are not suitable for amenities. On the gate, there is a posting with the name of a security
company, but other postings of rules were not found. Three points are hence
given for the dimension of maintenance.

In terms of accessibility, the POPS along the riverside is currently blocked
by fences and two gates, both of which are currently closed. Without a key, no
one can enter the POPS. The small POPS on the west border of the area is physically but not visually accessible, as it is far from the sidewalk and one must
cross the courtyard to get there. It is worth remembering here that this POPS
is intended for the potential continuation of the promenade with neighbouring property in the future. POPS as a pedestrian space is open to the public.
However, since physical accessibility in POPS Case 5 is generally low, only one
point is given. Visual accessibility is adequate; hence, three points are given.

For inclusiveness, the POPS as a pedestrian space is used for walking. The
POPS along the riverside is used for sitting, taking a break and having a conversation since there are amenities for these purposes. Due to its location,
people can also enjoy the river view. This POPS is large enough to accommodate other uses. As it is an open space without a roof, it may be used less
during the winter. Due to the closure, however, it was impossible to observe
who was actually using the area and how. Hence, two points are given for this
dimension.

Figure 7.18 Evaluation of POPS Case 5

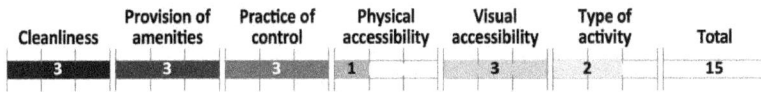

Cleanliness	Provision of amenities	Practice of control	Physical accessibility	Visual accessibility	Type of activity	Total
3	3	3	1	3	2	15

Source: Author's own figure.

Table 7.5 Information for POPS Case 5

Address	Holzmarktstr. 34
Building use	Apartment, office, hotel, retail and restaurants
POPS type	Plaza/pedestrian space
POPS size	-
Amenities	Bench, planting, lighting, litter receptacle

Source: Author's own table.

Figure 7.19 POPS Case 5 site map

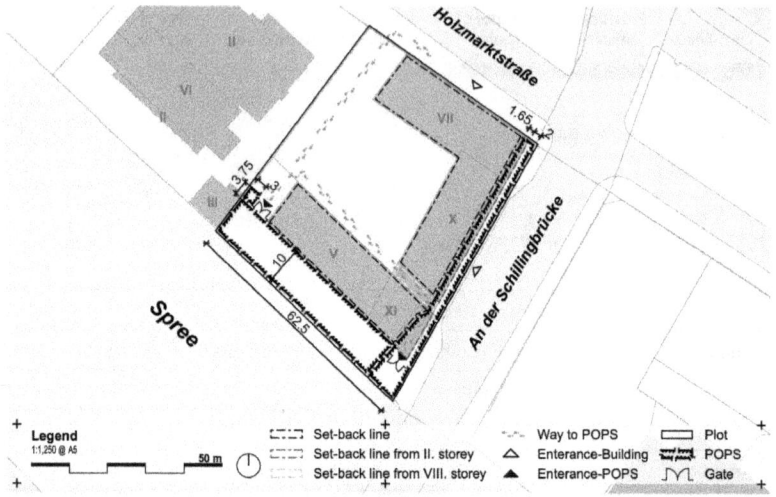

Source: Author's own figure based on B-Plan V-61.

Figure 7.20a Photographs for POPS Case 5: POPS along the river

Source: Author's own photo.

Figure 7.20b, c Photographs for POPS Case 5: Amenities provided on POPS and fence and locked gate to POPS

Source: Author's own photos.

Figure 7.20d, e Photographs for POPS Case 5: Security sign and POPS as pedestrian space

Source: Author's own photos.

7.2.2.   POPS Case 6: Mercedes-Benz Arena

This section involves an analysis of B-Plan V-3 and its explanatory statement.[2] The site covers an area of 18.2 hectares across the plots of Mühlenstraße 4–11, 31–33 and a partial plot of Mühlenstraße 12–30 on the Friedrichshain side. The area is bordered by railway tracks and a multi-purpose event hall to the north and Mühlenstraße with East-Side-Gallery to the south. The former Postbahnhof is located to the west; Warschauer Straße and the western boundary of buildings on Warschauer Straße to the east. The area is characterised by its inner-city location, its proximity to the historic centre and Alexanderplatz, as well as good connection to public transportation, offering 'the largest land potential' in this district (Bezirksamt FHKR von Berlin, 2004d).

Figure 7.21 Stipulations in graphic form regarding non-coverable areas in POPS Case 6

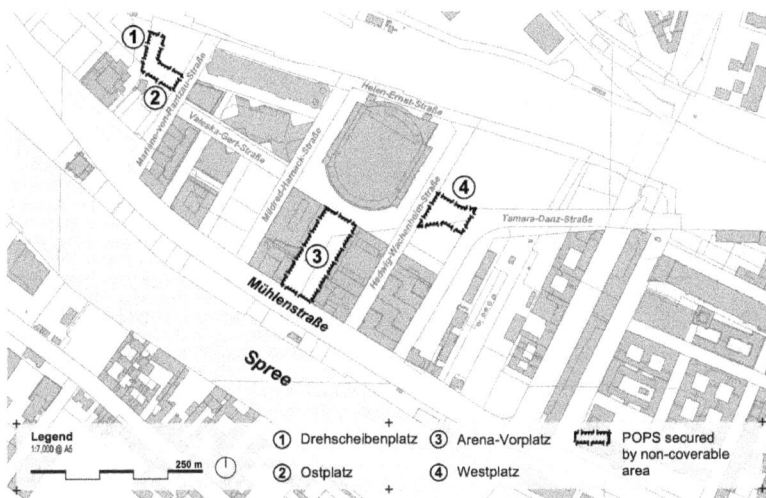

Source: Author's own figure based on B-Plan V-3.

---

2   See Bezirksamt FHKR von Berlin, 2004b, 2004d.

The area is the former East-side freight yard, consisting predominantly of disused areas. The site is characterised by railway facilities, logistic uses and inconsistent building structures. Railway operations ceased in September 2002 when the Federal Railway Authority released the area from railway use. The abandonment of its original use after reunification required the area to be reorganised and integrated into the planning of the wider area.

The majority of the planned area belongs to AEG: the American investor acquired the former railway property from DB AG and DB Netz AG to erect a multi-purpose event hall at its centre (already erected) and to develop the surrounding area (under construction, based on 2018). This is planned as a multi-use development, including sport, entertainment, retail, gastronomy and music, as well as office work and living coupled with a high density population. The development shall contribute significantly to the upgrading of the district and the city. Five instruments are used here in terms of POPS: non-coverable area, easement, urban development contract, green stipulation, and public and public authority participation.

Several non-coverable areas are marked out on the site (see Figure 7.21). The relatively dense development of the Mercedes-Benz Arena envisages a number of squares in the planned area. Aside from one publicly owned playground (Quartiersplatz), four POPS are planned: Drehscheibenplatz, Ostplatz, Arena-Vorplatz and Westplatz. These are to be created not in traffic areas but in non-coverable areas determined by building line, set-back line and coverage depth (in this case, the border of the road). Arena-Vorplatz will play a particular role as a bridge between the planned area and the riverside.

Moreover, public right of way is established for non-coverable areas (see Figure 7.22), that is, Drehscheibenplatz, Ostplatz, Arena-Vorplatz and Westplatz (see written stipulation no. 19). In addition, public right of way is set for Planstraße A (see written stipulation no. 21). Public right of way is supposed to be entered in the land registry as easement.

Stipulations in textual form regarding easement for POPS Case 6

- **No. 19:** Public right of way is set for the areas R, S1, S2 and T.
- **No. 21:** Public right of way is set for Planstraße A.

(Source: B-Plan V-3)

Figure 7.22 Stipulations in graphic form regarding easement for POPS Case 6

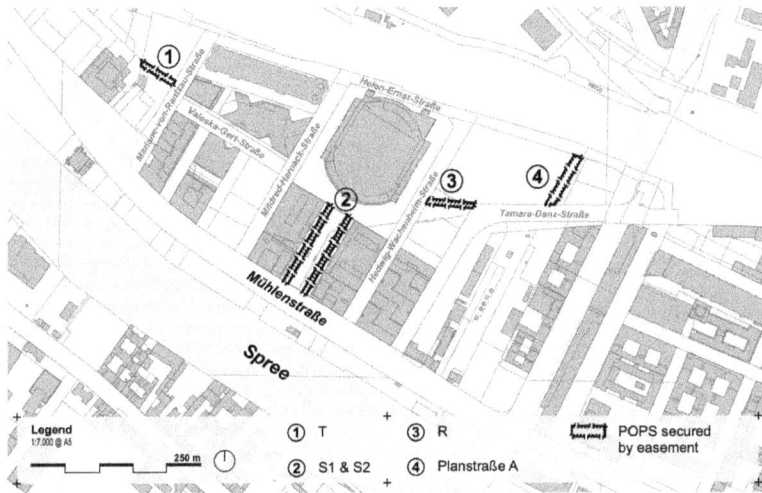

Source: Author's own figure based on B-Plan V-3.

In addition, an urban development contract was signed between the state of Berlin and the property owners AEG and BSR (see Figure 7.23). In terms of green space, this regulates the provision of a public playground (Quartiersplatz). Furthermore, it contains an arrangement on how to consider all plots of land on which public right of way has been arranged. According to the contract, private squares (Drehscheibenplatz, Ostplatz, Arena-Vorplatz and Westplatz) will remain under private ownership, and the respective owner will ensure that the public right of way is entered in the land registry. Furthermore, according to the urban development contract, the state of Berlin is obliged to acquire riverbank area through funds provided by AEG and BSR and to create public green space there. The city shall also use the funds to refurbish Rummelsburger Platz.

Green stipulation is also established (see Figure 7.24). As a counterbalance to the expected impact on nature and landscape due to construction, roofs within the area shall be extensively greened to a total of 18,900 square metres. Parts of the core area with high-rises are excluded from this arrangement (see written stipulation no. 22). A substrate layer of up to 5 cm is often used for the extensive greening of roofs, while the roofs themselves are to be designed in a way that is suitable for planting. In the core areas MK4.1a-d, MK4.2a-c, MK5, MK6.3 and MK6.4, green roofs are established to counteract exceeding the limit on the amount of land use set out in § 17 (1) BauNVO. Green roofs are not established in other parts of the core area, since they are adjacent to squares.

Figure 7.23 Stipulations in graphic form regarding urban development contract at Mercedes-Benz Arena

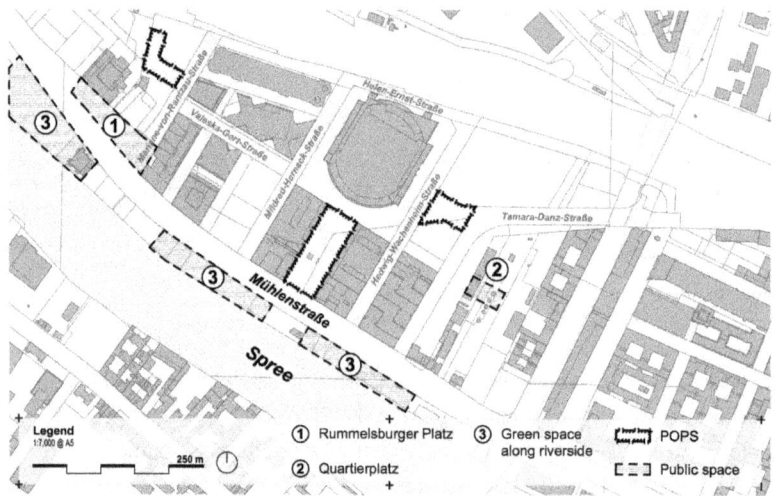

Source: Author's own figure based on explanatory statement V-3.

Stipulations in textual form regarding green stipulation for POPS Case 6

· **No. 22:** In the core area, aside from MK1, MK3, MK8.1 and MK8.2, roofs are to be extensively greened and maintained (at least 20% of coverable area).

· **No. 23:** In MK4.1a-d, MK4.2a-c, MK5, MK6.3 and MK6.4, the roofs are to be extensively greened and maintained (at least 10% of coverable area).

(Source: B-Plan V-3)

Figure 7.24 Stipulations in graphic form regarding green stipulation for POPS Case 6

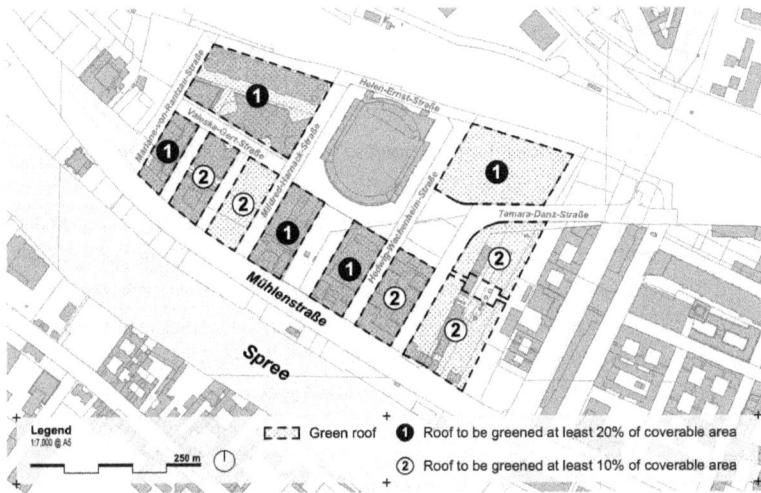

Source: Author's own figure based on B-Plan V-3.

Apart from the green stipulations set out in B-Plan V-3, replacement planting is to be arranged as an obligation within the urban development contract (see below).

Replacement planting

To fulfil the obligation of replacement planting pursuant to § 5 BaumSchVO, AEG undertakes to plant at least 211 trees in the planned area or in the area B-Plan 2-4VE. BSR undertakes to plant at least 11 trees in the planned area as well. If, for some reason, this is not possible, a countervailing charge of €900 is to be paid for each unplanted tree.

(Source: Explanatory statement V-3, p. 88)

Finally, public and public authority participation resulted in issues relevant to these POPS. Several suggestions were made during the early public and public authority participation concerning the content and impact of the plan. The suggestions relevant to POPS are provided in Figures 7.27 and 7.28 below.

The suggestion from the public was rejected, whereas the suggestion from a public authority was accepted.

Suggestion made during early public participation and result of weighing relevant to POPS Case 6

- **Suggestion:** Provide green and open space in favour of the residential area to the north of the railway facilities.
- **Weighing:** The area serves as a core area with predominantly commercial and cultural uses and contains only a small proportion of living spaces. The planned area is closed off from the residential area to the north by railway tracks and high-traffic roads. Public green space is available at the riverside. To improve the visual relationship with the river as well as ventilation, the East Side Gallery is to be opened opposite Arena-Vorplatz.

(Source: Explanatory statement V-3, pp. 94-95)

Suggestion made during early public authority participation and result of weighing relevant to POPS Case 6

- **Suggestion:** Consider the overall compensation concept when designating areas for greening measures outside the B-Plan.
- **Weighing:** In addition to measures determined in the B-Plan, further measures are planned to release and create vegetation areas and to provide route connections to integrate the riverside into the green and open space network. The establishment of measures is made partly by written stipulations in the B-Plan, partly in the urban development contract, and partly by securing funds via the urban development contract.

(Source: Explanatory statement V-3, p. 96)

Public display took place over the course of one month, and nine suggestions were received in total (four from the public, five from public authorities). The lack of green and open space was criticised several times. As a result, a distinction was made between the need for near-residential green space and near-settlement green space. It was also noted that the district of

Friedrichshain is generally undersupplied with green space and that no further green space is planned for the redevelopment of Warschauer Straße – another project nearby. (Below, Suggestion 1 came from the representative of the Warschauer Straße project.)

Suggestions made during formal public and public authority participation and results of weighing relevant to POPS Case 6

· **Suggestion 1:** The reservation of green space in the planned area as a potential compensation area.

· **Weighing 1:** The planned area is not suitable for the provision of near-residential green space and playground for the Warschauer Straße redevelopment due to its location, the barrier effect of railway tracks, the insufficient connection and the relatively long distance. On the other hand, for near-settlement green space, the realisation of high-quality public green space on the bank of the river Spree can contribute to a considerable relief of the strained situation in the surrounding area, even if the size does not meet the minimum requirement for near-settlement green space. The areas of Wriezener Bahnhof and the riverside are mentioned as potential compensation areas for new construction projects, although they would not reduce the existing green space deficits.

· **Suggestion 2:** More provision of green and open space in the planned area.

· **Weighing 2:** The provision of green and open space in the planned area is not only counteracted by private interests but also by superordinate plans, which envisage a lively urban quarter for working, living, shopping and entertainment, as well as public interests in upgrading an area that has been fallow and underused.

The fact that the areas designated as public green space in the planned area are insufficient to meet the needs is addressed both by the representative of the Warschauer Straße redevelopment and by Berliner Landesarbeitsgemeinschaft Naturschutz (hereafter BLN). In this context, the demand for approximately 10,000 m² of near-residential green space and 12,000 m² of near-settlement green space – calculated based on the guideline of the Deutscher Städtetag in Berlin – is compared only with the public playground whose area is 2,000 m². This calculation does not, however, include 5,500 m² of greenery roof that is to be provided according to the written stipulation. Rummelsburger Platz, which is set as a traffic area for administrative reasons but whose existing green space should be preserved and upgraded, is not included either. Moreover, the quality of the public playground is improved by a higher proportion of residential space around the playground and on Planstraße B, and by exclusion of large-scale retail, entertainment facilities and a petrol station. What is more, POPS within the planned area should be regarded as open space. In addition, further public green and open space is secured on the bank of the Spree through the binding land-use plan V-74.

The BLN points out that instead of the previously assumed 1,710 people, up to 3,040 residents could live in the planned area; hence, the demand for green and open space as well as playground should be set higher. A population of 1,710 is estimated based on the mandatory share of residential space (i.e., 90,000 m²). The total number of 3,040 inhabitants in the area is somewhat theoretical. It should be said that reference values are to be used as a benchmark for residential areas but not for core areas as, for core areas, fulfilling the mandatory residential space only is often the case. It is possible that significantly fewer families with children would live in this core area than on average.

(Source: Explanatory statement V-3, pp. 101-102)

Through public and public authority participation, the plan has been amended for the area of public playground at Quartiersplatz. Here, a relatively high concentration of housing is envisaged, while large-scale retail, entertainment facilities and a petrol station are excluded to upgrade the quality of the playground and promote living with children. The amendment of the draft B-Plan (with cover page from November 11, 2003), including the explanatory statement and environmental report, was subject to a new public display between December 1 and December 15, 2003. Within this time, suggestions could only be made regarding the changes to the draft plan. Altogether, seven written comments were received (four from citizens, three from public authorities), but no changes to the plan ensued.

**Suggestion made during second-round formal public participation and re-
sult of weighing relevant to POPS Case 6**

- **Suggestion:** The lack of green space within the planned area would be ex-
  acerbated by the increase in residential space around the playground at
  Quartiersplatz. Hence, the playground should be larger.
- **Weighing:** The amended B-Plan does not entail an increase in the number
  of residents. Rather, it only changed the distribution of the mandatory residential space within the planned area. Hence, there is no need for larger
  green space. Moreover, the shape of Quartiersplatz is the result of a report
  from expert review procedure. Thus, it should be maintained.

(Source: Explanatory statement V-3, p. 111)

Figure 7.25 Photograph of Mercedes-Benz Arena, 2018

Source: Author's own photo.

Since the POPS are yet to be completed, they could not be visited and evaluated (based on 2018).

Figure 7.26 POPS Case 6 site map

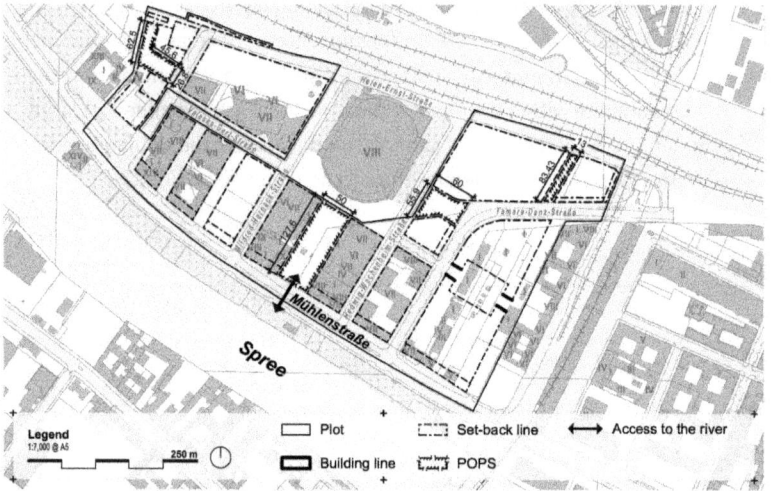

Source: Author's own figure based on B-Plan V-3.

7.2.3.   POPS Case 7: Köpenicker Str. 16–17

This section involves an analysis of B-Plan 2-7 and its explanatory statement.[3] This area, the former loading and docking area, is located north of Köpenicker Straße and is bordered by Brommystraße to the east, the river Spree to the north and the properties at Köpenicker Straße 18-20 to the west. Several buildings are located within the site, and it is a mixed-use area (mainly commercial, partly residential). Part of the courtyard space is used as parking space.

Figure 7.27 Stipulations in graphic form regarding easement in POPS Case 7

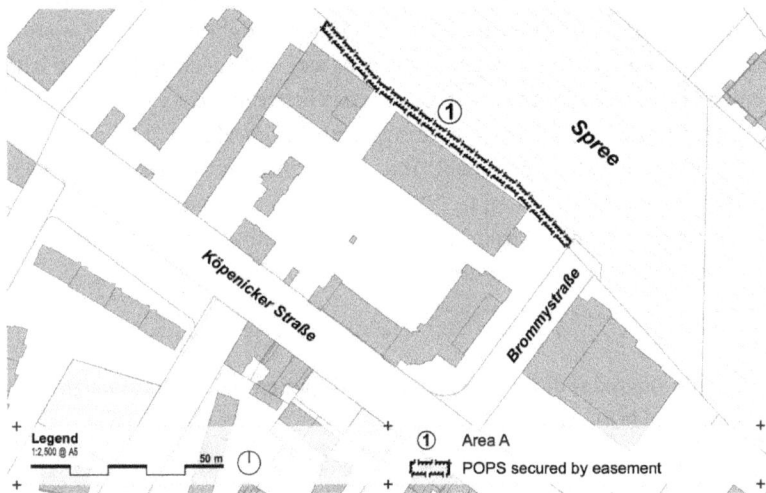

Source: Author's own figure based on B-Plan 2-7.

---

3   See Bezirksamt FHKR von Berlin, 2004a, 2004c.

Stipulations in textual form regarding easement in POPS Case 7

·   **No. 3:** Public right of way is set for area A.

(Source: B-Plan 2-7)

In terms of easement, POPS is provided on the riverside. The only stipulation made here in the sense of restrained planning is the public right of way (see Figure 7.27). The designation of green space depicted in the FNP is not subject to stipulation due to conservation issues in the area. Instead, public right of way is established to secure space for the creation of a riverside path. A five-metre-wide open space is secured through public right of way (see written stipulation no. 3). Granting public right of way and securing it in the land registry is written into the purchase contract between the state of Berlin and Heeresbäckerei Immobilienverwaltungs GmbH & Co. KG.

Apart from easement, public and public authority participation high-lighted several issues related to POPS. During the early public participation, suggestions were made regarding the riverside path. These suggestions and the results of their weighing are listed and summarised below:

Suggestions made during early public participation and results of weighing relevant to POPS Case 7

·   **Suggestion 1:** The riverside path should be open 24/7 via the public right of way.
·   **Weighing 1:** The goal is to provide a riverside path without restriction over-all. However, time of use (opening hours) cannot be established in the B-Plan due to the lack of a legal basis.
·   **Suggestion 2:** The riverside path should be 10 m wide instead of 5 m to allow pedestrians and cyclists to run/ride side-by-side without conflict.
·   **Weighing 2:** The overall concept for providing a riverside path along the Kreuzberg side of the Spree indicates 10 m as the standard width. How-

ever, each site has specific circumstances to consider. In this case, a five-metre-wide riverside path is set due to conservation issues.

(Source: Explanatory statement 2-7, pp. 11-12)

POPS Case 7 was visited three times during the day in November 2017 as well as in May and July 2018. In terms of maintenance, the POPS is usable, clean and safe. It has no fly tipping or fly posting, nor any posting of sets of rules. However, it does not provide any amenities. Thus, three points are given for cleanliness and practice of control, but only one point is given for the provision of amenities.

This POPS has a low level of accessibility, both physically and visually. The site is surrounded by a wall, and one must enter a gate and cross a courtyard to gain access. It is also invisible from the adjacent street, and since there is nothing to signify it as a POPS, it is unlikely that people would go there without prior knowledge. Moreover, the riverside path that is designated as POPS is interrupted by a restaurant in the middle, meaning it is only open during the opening hours of the restaurant (from evening to night only, based on 2018). Outside of these hours, this part of the POPS cannot be accessed at all; during these hours, it can only be accessed by guests of the restaurant. Hence, one point is given for both physical and visual accessibility.

Turning to inclusiveness, since the POPS is very narrow (i.e., a five-metre-wide path along the river; see Figure 7.27), it is unlikely that any activity can take place. Also, the area of the POPS used by the restaurant is not inclusive at all since it is mostly closed. Due to its proximity to the river, however, people who know this place seem to visit, sit directly at the edge and enjoy their time (see Figure 7.30). This may be possible during the opening hours of the restaurant from evening to night when more people are present within the site. However, even if this is the case, this POPS is not considered to be inclusive: although it may be used by people who work within the site, by guests of the restaurant or by people who already know the area, the lack of amenities and accessibility means it is unlikely to attract a wide range of people. Hence, one point is given for inclusiveness.

Figure 7.28 Evaluation of POPS Case 7

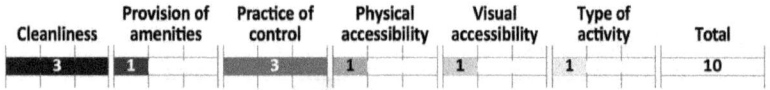

Cleanliness	Provision of amenities	Practice of control	Physical accessibility	Visual accessibility	Type of activity	Total
3	1	3	1	1	1	10

Source: Author's own figure.

Table 7.6 Information for POPS Case 7

Address	Köpenicker Str. 16-17
Building use	(Mainly) commercial use
POPS type	Plaza
POPS size	-
Amenities	None

Source: Author's own table.

Figure 7.29 POPS Case 7 site map

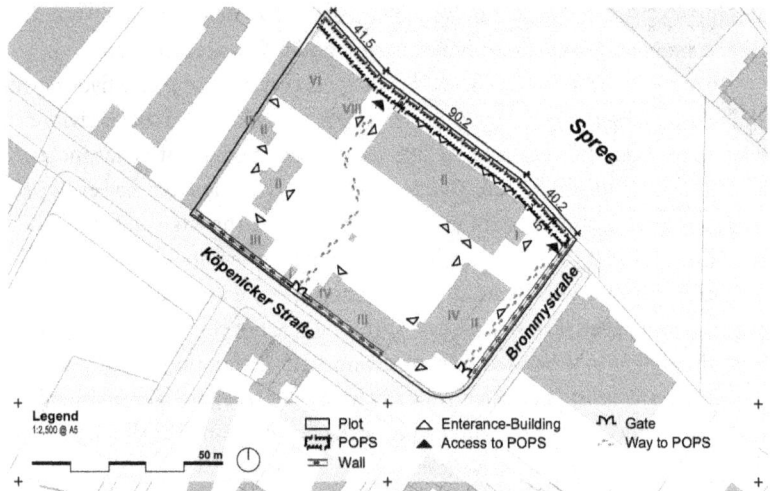

Source: Author's own figure based on B-Plan 2-7.

Figure 7.30a Photographs for POPS Case 7: POPS – only the five-metre-wide path along the river. The large empty space is not designated as POPS

Source: Author's own photo.

Figure 7.30b, c Photographs for POPS Case 7: Building site and gate to access to POPS

Source: Author's own photos.

Figure 7.30d, e Photographs for POPS Case 7: POPS as riverside path space and POPS used by restaurant (gate closed outside opening hours)

Source: Author's own photos.

7.2.4.   POPS Case 8: Pfuelstr./Köpenicker Str.

This section involves an analysis of B-Plan VI-146 and its explanatory statement.[4] For Case 8, the site in which B-Plan is established is located to the north of Köpenicker Straße and bordered by Pfuelstraße to the east, the river Spree to the north and an undeveloped plot (Köpenicker Straße 11–12) to the west. The area is densely built with old buildings of up to six stories, and the area is mixed-use. Buildings along Köpenicker Straße are mainly used for residential purposes, while the ground floor is partly occupied by retail and office space. Buildings along the riverside are mainly used for industrial purposes.

Public easement is established on the riverside (see Figure 7.31). Within the existing building structure, this was the only place that was open to the river. In contrast to previous cases, B-Plan VI-146 does not require any public access; there was no need since public easement had already been established at Köpeniker Straße 8.

Figure 7.31 Stipulations in graphic form regarding public easement for POPS Case 8

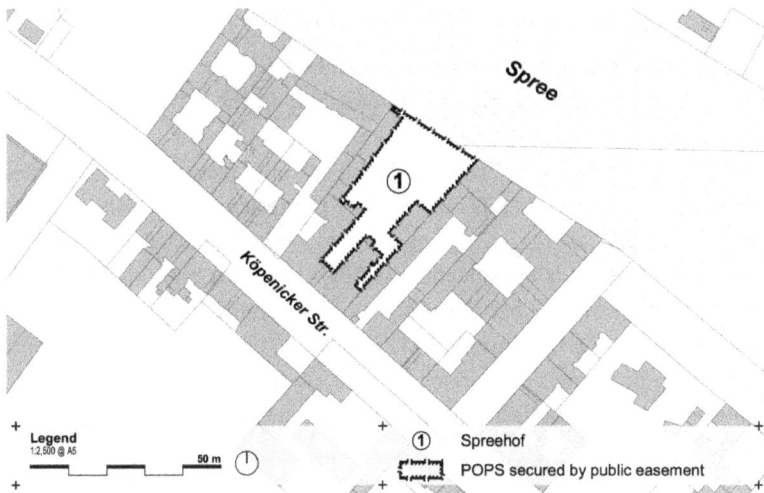

Source: Author's own figure based on explanatory statement VI-146.

---

4   see Bezirksamt FHKR von Berlin, 2005a, 2005b.

In addition to public easement, public and public authority participation highlighted certain issues related to POPS. A concept was introduced in the early public participation, featuring the riverside path with public right of way. Two citizens took part, one of whom welcomed the premise of right of way along the riverside. However, this idea was abandoned as it would involve the demolition of buildings and cost-intensive intervention in private property.

Here, a POPS named Spreehof is provided for all. This POPS was visited three times during the day in November 2017 as well as in May and July 2018. In terms of maintenance, it is usable, clean and safe. It does not have fly tipping or posting, and amenities are kept to desired standards. Various amenities are provided, including a bench, a litter receptacle, a small playground and a basketball court. There is one posting of rules, which states that dogs are not allowed to enter. Other than that, there are no rules. Hence, three points are given for this dimension.

Regarding accessibility, the area is less accessible due to the gate. It is not clearly visible from the street and, although there is signage indicating Spreehof, it is somewhat unclear whether it is accessible to all due to its character as a courtyard. The door is also closed. As a result, only one point is given for this dimension.

For inclusiveness, this POPS can accommodate several activities like sitting, taking a break, and playing basketball or in the playground. Indeed, the amenities invite a wide range of people – from children and teenagers to adults. However, as this is a courtyard with a gate and low accessibility, there is a danger that this POPS is only used by the residents and visitors of the buildings. In fact, every time during the field work, no one was present. Due to residential use, it is unlikely that the POPS is busy at night. Nevertheless, due to its large size, it has the potential to accommodate different activities and to attract a wide range of the population if accessibility is improved and some programmes were organised and held there. Taking everything into consideration, two points are given for inclusiveness.

Figure 7.32 Evaluation of POPS Case 8

Cleanliness	Provision of amenities	Practice of control	Physical accessibility	Visual accessibility	Type of activity	Total
3	3	3	1	1	2	13

Source: Author's own figure.

Table 7.7 Information for POPS Case 8

Address	Pfuelstr./Köpenicker Str.
Building use	Living, office, retail
POPS type	Garden
POPS size	-
Amenities	Bench, litter receptacle, small playground and basketball stand

Source: Author's own table.

Figure 7.33 POPS Case 8 site map

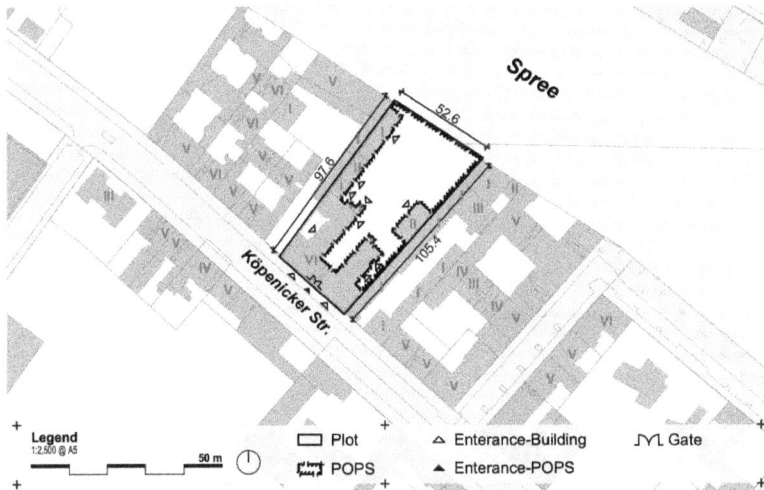

Source: Author's own figure based on explanatory statement VI-146.

Figure 7.34a Photographs for POPS Case 8: POPS during the day

Source: Author's own photo.

Figure 7.34b, c Photographs for POPS Case 8: Playground and courtyard

Source: Author's own photos.

Figure 7.34d, e Photographs for POPS Case 8: Gate to POPS and sign at the gate indicating Spreehof

Source: Author's own photos.

7.3.   Conclusion

Altogether, eight POPS in Teheran-ro and Mediaspree area were visited and analysed, seven of which were evaluated to better understand the respective planning instruments and their consequences. In turn, three key dimensions of publicness of public space were used as part of this evaluation: maintenance, accessibility and inclusiveness. Figure 7.35 shows the results of the evaluation of POPS in both Teheran-ro and Mediaspree area.

First, the findings for POPS in Teheran-ro are presented and interpreted in relation to the planning instruments explained in Chapter 5. In terms of cleanliness, all four POPS received three points. This can be interpreted as the result of efforts by both the public and private sectors. As explained in Chapter 5, the public sector's approach to POPS has shifted from provision to management. Whether POPS are well maintained is verified by the public sector through regular inspection. On the other hand, owners are also willing to keep POPS clean as they are located directly in front of or at the corner of their buildings (or connected to their entrances) and therefore act as the face of the building.

The selected POPS in Teheran-ro generally have a good provision of amenities to encourage activities like sitting, taking a break, chatting or smoking. Initially, POPS may look uniform due to the provision of similar types of amenities. Yet, the site visit and analysis revealed that the type of amenities and degree of provision vary depending on the type of POPS – generally, garden- and plaza-type POPS are better equipped than pedestrian spaces. It can be inferred that different uses are intended depending on the type of POPS, so that pedestrian space, for instance, is typically seen as a place to pass through. Garden and plaza types of POPS, on the other hand, are well equipped with amenities like benches and planting. This can be seen as the result of regulation on amenities; as explained in Chapter 5, all planning instruments at the city level regulate the provision of amenities in greater detail. Moreover, all POPS provide signage to inform people that they are there to be used. This may also be due to regulation; indeed, the importance of signage has increased recently to the point that POPS must now feature at least one signage.

In terms of practice of control, POPS in Teheran-ro are characterised by a mid-to-low level of control. Where sets of rules are posted, they are limited to informing users that smoking is forbidden. According to the expert interviews and my own observations, smoking seems to be a real issue in POPS, especially clashes between smokers and non-smokers. Hence, this rule was not seen as something that decreases publicness; rather, it attempts to regulate how POPS should be used. Despite all buildings having security guards, according to the observation, they were less present outside buildings. However, where there were additional signs indicating 24/7 camera surveillance, one point was deducted as this may increase the sense of control in combination with the presence of a security guard.

Concerning accessibility, both physical and visual accessibility is generally high in POPS in Teheran-ro, although there is one case (POPS Case 4) where access is somewhat difficult. In this case, the owner has provided another POPS in front of the building in the form of pedestrian space, which may be seen as adequate compensation. In all the other cases, accessibility is high. This may be seen as the result of emphasis on the location of POPS, which is regulated by all planning instruments at the city level. One of the interviewees also confirmed that, in practice, the accessibility to (and therefore location of) POPS is regarded as the most important aspect during the review process. What is more, none of the selected POPS in Teheran-ro are blocked or used for private purposes. This may be interpreted as the result of regular inspection.

In terms of inclusiveness, the POPS in Teheran-ro present different results. The inclusiveness of POPS depends on their maintenance, accessibility and size. Whereas maintenance and accessibility are generally good, these POPS are not large enough to host various activities, especially when divided into two. Interestingly, however, the division of POPS does not always negatively impact inclusiveness, as evidenced by POPS Case 3. Here, the division allows different uses to be accommodated (including for non-smokers), thereby resolving potential conflict between users. The site visit and analysis also revealed that inclusiveness can also depend on other factors, such as surrounding land uses. Whereas Cases 1 and 3 are similar in terms of quality, Case 3 attracts a wider range of people. This could be due to the division of the POPS or to surrounding uses: POPS Case 3 is located next to a residential area, whereas POPS Case 1 is surrounded by office and commercial use and is hence restricted to office workers.

In summary, POPS in Teheran-ro are generally clean, well equipped, semi-controlled and accessible. They are inclusive to varying degrees. This means that they have the potential to be used actively, but it is less likely that one POPS can accommodate several activities at once, a notion reinforced by my own observations. That said, as explained in Chapter 5, the main purpose of planning instruments in Teheran-ro is to secure walking space and resting areas as well as to promote use – and not necessarily to accommodate various uses.

The following section presents the evaluation results for POPS in Mediaspree area and interprets them in relation to the planning instruments explained in Chapter 6. In terms of cleanliness, all four of the selected POPS received three points. This can be interpreted as the result of efforts by the public and/or private sector, depending on the arrangement since the city and building owners agree on who is responsible for cleaning POPS (and responsibility can be shared). This is arranged by urban development contracts. As this information is not open to the public, however, it was impossible to check in any finer detail. Nevertheless, it is evident that owners are willing to keep POPS clean, as low-quality outdoor space would give a bad impression to visitors. The public sector is also willing to keep POPS clean to uphold quality.

Figure 7.35 Comparative evaluation of POPS in Teheran-ro and Mediaspree area

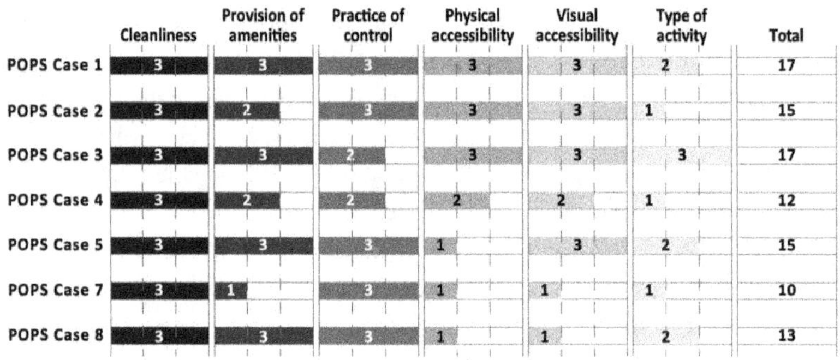

	Cleanliness	Provision of amenities	Practice of control	Physical accessibility	Visual accessibility	Type of activity	Total
POPS Case 1	3	3	3	3	3	2	17
POPS Case 2	3	2	3	3	3	1	15
POPS Case 3	3	3	2	3	3	3	17
POPS Case 4	3	2	2	2	2	1	12
POPS Case 5	3	3	3	1	3	2	15
POPS Case 7	3	1	3	1	1	1	10
POPS Case 8	3	3	3	1	1	2	13

Source: Author's own figure.

Regarding amenities, the POPS in Mediaspree area display contrasting results. Two out of three are well equipped, while one has no amenities at all. The decisive factor here seems to be the size of the POPS. In other words, POPS Case 7 has no amenities because it simply has no room to put them. POPS Case 8, on the other hand, has adequate space and provides a wide range of amenities from benches to playgrounds. Surrounding use may also be a significant factor here: whereas POPS Case 7 is surrounded by office and commercial uses, POPS Case 8 is also surrounded by, among others, residential use. As a result, the presence of residents means greater demand for community space.

In terms of practice of control, there is a low degree of control in Mediaspree area. POPS Case 5 includes a security company sign at the gate, and the gate for POPS Case 8 displays a sign that dogs are not allowed to enter. No surveillance cameras or security guards were observed.

Concerning accessibility, both physical and visual accessibility is generally poor in Mediaspree area. POPS Case 5 is closed from public use, while POPS Case 8 features a gate that makes the POPS invisible and gives the impression of a private space. POPS Case 7 is also difficult to access as it is surrounded by a wall and requires users to cross over a courtyard. Moreover, half of the POPS is only accessible during the opening hours of the on-site restaurant, which is from evening to night (based on 2018). Indeed, one of the suggestions made during public and public authority participation was to open the POPS Case 7 24/7, but the response from the public sector was that the opening hours could not be set in the B-Plan due to a lack of legal basis. In short, unless people already know the areas, POPS Case 7 and 8 would not be visited. Equally, the fact that POPS Case 5 is closed to public use can be interpreted as the result of the absence of inspection. Although the location of POPS is the most frequently regulated aspect, as explained in Chapter 6, it seems that planning instruments have been effective in securing public access to the river Spree but less effective in encouraging accessibility. This could be partly due to existing building structures; at the same time, it seems that whether POPS are well connected to the main street so that people may see and use them is generally less discussed.

The POPS in Mediaspree area also present different results regarding inclusiveness. Whereas the selected POPS are generally well maintained, they are less accessible. Less accessibility means that POPS cannot be visited or used by a wide range of people. The size of POPS also differs greatly: while POPS Case 8 is large and enables various activities, POPS Case 7 is too small to host any such activities. As argued above in relation to the provision of amenities, surrounding use may also have an effect on inclusiveness.

In summary, the selected POPS in Mediaspree area are generally clean and less controlled, but they are also less accessible. This suggests that they have different potentials for use. Perhaps unsurprisingly, given that planning instruments are exercised on a case-by-case basis, the outcomes all appear to be different as well. As explained in Chapter 6, one of the driving purposes behind planning instruments in Mediaspree area is to secure public access to the river. As reflected in reality, this has been achieved, yet the quality of the resulting POPS varies significantly.

Chapter 8. Conclusion

This closing chapter is structured based on the four research questions. The first three subchapters summarise the answers to the first three research questions, while the book ends with a number of policy recommendations for cities undergoing radical transformation and facing high development pressure, whose officers are searching for ways to engage other stakeholders, including the private sector, in public space provision and management (i.e., the subject of the fourth research question).

8.1. Answer to the first research question

The first research question asks: What challenges does the public sector face in providing and managing public space in a transitional context?

Public space is a multi-dimensional concept with a range of possible dimensions, such as ownership, maintenance, accessibility and inclusiveness. Public spaces are produced by and within a society; just as society keeps changing, they too evolve constantly. The cases of Teheran-ro and Mediaspree area reveal that changes in public space are even more remarkable in transitional contexts and that common issues around public space arise when cities undergo radical transformation and have high development pressure.

Although the drivers of transformation in Teheran-ro and Mediaspree area are different, they face the same challenge of public sector incapacity to provide and manage public space alone, especially in a transitional context. In Seoul, the rapid development of Teheran-ro in the process of urban expansion and population growth resulted in a low-quality urban environment. Although a large amount of public space was needed in order to provide enough walking space and resting area for the public, the public sector was unable to provide and manage public space alone due to rapidly increasing land values.

In Berlin, which underwent radical changes after the fall of socialism and the subsequent German reunification, securing public access to the riverside as well as providing public space within the Mediaspree area have proven to be major challenges. In response, the public sector was neither willing nor capable to (re)purchase private land due to the city's difficult financial situation, as well as the social imperatives for deregulation and market liberalisation.

8.2.   Answer to the second research question

The second research question asks: How does the public sector address these challenges?

To respond to the challenge of providing and managing public space, in both cases the public sector has actively engaged the private sector to share costs, rights and responsibilities regarding public space provision and management. In fact, both Teheran-ro and Mediaspree area have exercised planning instruments to engage the private sector in the form of POPS. The relevant planning instruments in Teheran-ro differ from those used in Mediaspree area in several aspects. These are compared in the following section.

8.2.1.   Comparing planning instruments
for regulating provision of POPS

Public sector officials are active in regulating the provision of POPS in both Teheran-ro and Mediaspree area. The first two subcategories of provision, zoning and facility, relate to where to provide POPS. In the case of Teheran-ro, POPS are not supposed to be provided everywhere but are legally required to be provided in certain zones as regulated by the Building Act. Whether the building is in a certain use and whether its total floor area exceeds 5,000 square metres are the deciding factors; if both conditions are met, POPS are legally required. In Mediaspree area, by contrast, it is the local circumstances that prove decisive. The public sector can only demand POPS from building owners if there is a need for publicly accessible spaces within the wider neighbourhood. As elaborated in Chapter 6, a wide range of planning instruments from the upper level have provided evidence for the need for POPS in the area as well as suggestions on where they should be provided. The exact location of POPS is then regulated at the site level through instruments like non-coverable area, easement and public easement.

The location of POPS in Mediaspree area is regulated at different levels and, to be more precise, this is the only aspect that is widely addressed. Indeed, all the instruments examined (except for green stipulation) regulate the location of POPS. This suggests that the location of POPS is critical; in Mediaspree area, this is often riverside, as one of the main purposes of the respective planning instruments is to secure public access to the river. Location of POPS is also a crucial issue in Teheran-ro. For example, all instruments at the city level regulate the location of POPS to promote the use of POPS. The purpose of planning instruments for POPS has evolved from securing walking space and resting areas to promoting use. POPS that are adjacent to the main road are likely to attract users; hence, the location of POPS is significant.

In Teheran-ro, the type of POPS is addressed by all instruments at the city level, as it is another significant factor for promoting use. Instruments provide detailed information on which types of POPS are available and how they should be designed. These options include indoor POPS; although this type has not yet gained popularity, it has the potential for future promotion. Aside from the type of POPS, planning instruments in Teheran-ro also regulate the number and dimensions of POPS. In Mediaspree area, a design guideline suggests promenade as the most appropriate type of POPS along the river Spree. Uniform design is prioritised here to give a sense of continuity to the character of publicly useable space, regardless of its actual ownership. The type of POPS can also be discussed through public and public authority participation. Even though public and public authority participation is not legally binding, it nonetheless offers the opportunity for the public and public authorities to express their opinions and to debate topics such as (but not limited to) the number and dimensions of POPS and the amenities they feature.

Availability of amenities is another important aspect of POPS provision. In Teheran-ro, detailed legislations, standards and guidelines outline the types of amenities that should be provided in which types of POPS and how. In general, there is a far stronger focus on the design of POPS in Teheran-ro than in Mediaspree area. Among the various types of amenities, signage has gained great importance in Teheran-ro: all POPS include at least one signage. This is crucial, as people would not use the space if they were unsure about their rights to do so. In Mediaspree area, greening seems to be important: green stipulation is the instrument that provides detailed information on greening only (e.g., on the type of planting or about green roofs), although it is regulated differently. Provision of amenities can also be encompassed by urban development contracts or public and public authority participation, depending on the individual case. For each case, the design of POPS is subject to negotiation between the city and the building owners.

Incentives are another crucial aspect since favourable incentives can encourage owners to provide POPS. The fact that this is addressed by almost all the planning instruments in Teheran-ro would seem to prove its importance. In Teheran-ro, incentives are arranged according to a mathematical formula, whereas in Mediaspree area, they are arranged case-by-case through urban development contracts. In case of Teheran-ro, attempts have been made to make best use of incentives. The regulation has been changed; whereas previous incentives were only given to POPS in excess of the liable area, they are now given in line with the size of POPS installed.

8.2.2. Comparing planning instruments for regulating management of POPS

There are regulations for the management of POPS in both Teheran-ro and Mediaspree area. Management consists of five aspects: maintenance, financial support, inspection of POPS, infraction proceedings, and use of POPS. Maintenance is the responsibility of owners in Teheran-ro; planning instruments require owners to take both physical and financial responsibility for day-to-day maintenance. When it comes to renovation of POPS that are older than five years, the Seoul Ordinance on Building states that the public sector may provide financial resources. In Mediaspree area, owners are also generally responsible for maintenance, yet there can be exceptions depending on the arrangement between the city and the owners.

Turning to inspection and infraction proceedings, their aim is to check whether owners are compliant with the law so that POPS function as public space. Owners may choose to block POPS from public use and use them for private purposes. To prevent this, inspections are conducted every year in Teheran-ro, with fines imposed for non-compliance. These are the core planning instruments for the management of POPS in Teheran-ro. In contrast, there are no instruments for inspection and infraction proceedings in Mediaspree area.

Use of POPS is another aspect of management of POPS. After POPS are provided, their use should be promoted. Hence, planning instruments in Teheran-ro promote the use of POPS through a policy that allows others to use POPS for various purposes, such as holding an event. This is not the case in Mediaspree area; there is no instrument that explicitly promotes the use of POPS.

Ultimately, while both public sectors in these cases are equipped with numerous planning instruments for the provision of POPS, there is a huge difference in terms of which aspects are regulated and to what extent. Whereas the focus is mainly on location in Mediaspree area, all aspects – from zoning to incentives – are regulated to a greater extent in Teheran-ro. The planning instruments for Teheran-ro are best described as detailed and product-orientated. In contrast, planning instruments in Mediaspree area are best described as plan-focused and case-by-case. Another difference is in the level of planning instruments that have a direct impact on POPS. In Teheran-ro, both national- and city-level instruments directly influence each individual POPS; in Mediaspree area, they are restricted to the site level and are hence more site-specific. Another sizeable difference emerges in the management of POPS. For the most part, management of POPS is considered important in Teheran-ro. Indeed, the focus has shifted from the provision of POPS to their management, as underuse and private use of POPS have been persistent problems. In Mediaspree area, on the other hand, management of POPS is generally less regulated.

8.3.   Answer to the third research question

The third research question asks: What do the outcomes of the respective planning instruments look like in reality?

After each planning instrument was analysed, a total of eight POPS in Teheran-ro (four) and Mediaspree area (four) were visited, analysed and evaluated to better understand the planning instruments as well as their outcomes in real terms. The results are then compared based on maintenance (cleanliness, provision of amenities, practice of control), accessibility (physical/visual) and inclusiveness.

Maintenance of POPS consists of cleanliness, provision of amenities and practice of control. In terms of cleanliness, all the POPS visited in Teheran-ro and Mediaspree area were clean to a similar extent. They are usable, clean and safe, free from fly tipping or posting, and amenities are kept to desired standards. This is not surprising in the case of Teheran-ro, where owners are legally required to maintain POPS, as verified by the public sector through regular inspection. In Mediaspree area, meanwhile, this responsibility can belong to the city, the owners, or be shared between the two depending on the individual arrangement. In both cases, owners are willing to keep POPS clean to maintain a good impression of POPS as the "face" of their buildings, while the public sector is also willing to keep POPS clean to uphold quality.

POPS in Teheran-ro are generally well equipped in terms of amenities, although this is dependent on the type of POPS: generally speaking, garden and plaza types of POPS are better equipped than pedestrian spaces. The former are equipped with amenities like benches and planting, which encourage activities like sitting, taking a break and chatting. Although the pedestrian type of POPS may be less equipped, as one of the examples shows, this may be compensated by another POPS on the same site (in this case another type of POPS). Due to the detailed legislation, standards and guidelines on the provision of amenities, minimum quality is secured. In Mediaspree area, it seems that the larger POPS are, the better they are equipped, and that surrounding use plays a role.

Regarding the practice of control, POPS in Mediaspree area are generally less controlled than their equivalents in Teheran-ro. In both cases, sets of rules were posted, for example, to inform users not to smoke or not to allow dogs to enter. In Teheran-ro, all buildings have security guards, even though they are less present outside buildings. In addition, a number of POPS in Teheran-ro also have signs indicating that surveillance cameras are in use 24/7.

In terms of accessibility, both physical and visual accessibility is generally higher in Teheran-ro than in Mediaspree area. In the Seoul case, this may be seen as the result of emphasis on location of POPS in every planning instrument at the city level, as well as regular inspection to prevent blocking of POPS. In Mediaspree area, while the location of POPS is also widely addressed by various planning instruments, the outcome reveals that they are effective in securing public access to the river but less effective in encouraging accessibility. Two POPS out of the three visited are of a courtyard style surrounded by a wall or closed off with a gate. It appears that whether POPS are well connected to the main street so that people can see them and use them is less discussed. Also, one of the POPS visited is currently blocked from public use; this may be due to the absence of inspection and infraction proceedings.

Lastly, the site visits and analysis revealed that POPS in both Teheran-ro and Mediaspree area can vary drastically in their levels of inclusiveness. In Teheran-ro, given that POPS are generally well maintained and accessible, POPS have the potential to be inclusive. However, some POPS can be seen as less inclusive due to their small size, meaning it is difficult to host different activities. Similarly, in Mediaspree area, POPS are well maintained, which increases the likelihood that POPS are inclusive. However, due to the low level of accessibility, POPS are less inclusive. The size of POPS varies greatly as well.

8.4.   Answer to the fourth research question

The fourth research question asks: What implications does the research provide for cities undergoing rapid transformation and facing high development pressure, and which are looking for ways to engage other stakeholders, including the private sector, in public space provision and management?

Policy recommendations are drawn from the comparison of planning instruments (see 8.2) and their outcomes (see 8.3) in Teheran-ro and Mediaspree area. The uniqueness of the respective planning instruments – some of which constitute strengths or weaknesses – will be first elaborated followed by policy recommendations and implications for future research.

8.4.1.   Uniqueness of planning instruments in Teheran-ro and Mediaspree area

What is unique about planning instruments in Teheran-ro is that there are legislations, standards and guidelines devoted to POPS. These planning instruments provide detailed information on how POPS should be provided and managed. They are product-orientated, with a strong focus on design. These detailed legislations, standards and guidelines can be seen as both a strength and a weakness: minimum quality is guaranteed, but there is little room for manoeuvre. Indeed, planning instruments for POPS are not site-specific, and it would appear that the public sector is aware of criticisms over uniform space. Hence, it has tried to introduce more variation, for instance, by proposing different types of POPS.

Another uniqueness, compared to the instruments used in Mediaspree area, is that planning instruments in Teheran-ro not only try to secure space for walking and resting but go one step further to promote the actual use of POPS. Initially, emphasis was given to the provision of POPS, and the instruments were successful in the sense that many POPS were created. However, these POPS were of poor quality, and underuse and private use proved to be persistent problems. Hence, over the last decade, the public sector's focus has shifted from provision to active management, including attempts to promote the actual use of POPS. On the one hand, inspection and infraction proceedings help to prevent private use of POPS; on the other, recent policymaking has opened up the opportunity for POPS to be used for events.

Table 8.1 Uniqueness of planning instruments in Teheran-ro and Mediaspree area

	Teheran-ro	Mediaspree area
Provision of POPS	· Detailed legislations, standards and guidelines devoted to provision of POPS at national and city levels · Aspects of provision broadly covered from zoning to incentives · Planning instruments not site-specific · Product-orientated; strong focus on design · Little room for manoeuvre · Focus on increasing both quantity and quality so that POPS can be better used	· Provision of POPS depending on local circumstances · Site-specific planning instruments; plan-focused · Regulated on a case-by-case basis · Negotiation as central element · Strong focus on location of POPS · Possibility given for public and public authority to participate
Management of POPS	· Detailed legislation, standards and guidelines devoted to management of POPS at national and city levels · Inspection and policy to promote use of POPS as central element	· Management less regulated; lack of measures · No monitoring

Source: Author's own table.

In Mediaspree area, planning instruments have been effective in securing public access to private pieces of land. What is unique in this case is that the planning instruments are site-specific. Indeed, the upper-level planning instruments have no direct impact on the provision and management of individual POPS; rather, they only shape the decision-making environment and give justification for POPS. Those planning instruments that do have a direct impact come from the site level.

Another uniqueness is that the provision and management of POPS are regulated on a case-by-case basis. This can be seen as both a strength and a weakness since the quality of POPS can vary hugely. The case-by-case basis requires local planning officers to be competent; they also have to negotiate with owners, and this is not always easy. When it comes to large developments, they need to find the right balance between not requiring too much – otherwise they may lose investors – and securing POPS and ensuring their quality. Such negotiation results in, on one hand, greater flexibility and variation of POPS according to the local scenario and needs. On the other hand, the number and quality of POPS can be dependent on the competence of individual local planning officers. Hence, there is a danger that planning instruments are not used to their full extent but are, for instance, limited to securing public access only.

In addition, the uniqueness here lies in the lack of measures for managing POPS. Since POPS are not monitored, it is possible that some owners will choose not to comply with the law or honour their arrangement with the city. This would result in negative consequences, such as preventing public access to POPS or their diminished quality.

Lastly, people other than local planning officers and building owners can engage in the process and express their ideas and opinions regarding POPS. Although it is not devoted wholly to POPS and the results are not legally binding, giving the option can be beneficial.

8.4.2.   Policy recommendations

POPS are co-produced and co-managed public spaces where the public sector acts as the regulator and lawmaker while the private sector acts as the implementer. Planning instruments are crucial here as they directly impact how POPS are provided and managed. Policy recommendations are drawn from the research result to improve planning practice.

First, the engagement of private actors helps the public sector in public space provision and management. The involvement of private actors does not necessarily reduce the publicness of public space, as long as the roles and responsibilities in the provision and management of POPS are clarified and agreed upon with the public sector. This may already be established legally or defined through negotiation with the private sector. POPS is a powerful mechanism that can help achieve a high quantity and quality of urban public space, especially when the public sector is incapable of providing and managing public space alone.

Second, detailed guidelines on how POPS should be provided and managed are crucial to guarantee their quality. This may not be legally binding to allow for leeway. Likewise, the guidance should offer a wide range of variations – to prevent uniform POPS – and take the key dimensions of publicness of public space (i.e., maintenance, accessibility and inclusiveness) into account so that POPS can be of high quality and better used. As an example, the guideline may suggest installing signage at the entrance of POPS so that the public can recognise their right to access and use. This guideline may also be used as part of the review criteria if a city wants to make POPS more effective.

Third, the macro analysis is helpful for stakeholders in their decision-making on POPS. It provides information on, for example, how many POPS are needed in the neighbourhood, what types of POPS are needed, and their potential users. POPS can then be provided according to local circumstances and needs, as POPS that are site-specific have a better chance of being used.

Fourth, regular inspection is crucial to ensure ongoing compliance with the law or the arrangement made with the public sector. Any owners breaking the rules should be subject to penalty, and it is important that fines can be charged immediately; it is only then that the system can be effective in returning POPS to public use.

Fifth, regulation alone does not work; it needs to be balanced with incentives. Good incentives encourage building owners to provide high-quality POPS. Building-to-land ratio, floor area ratio and/or height limit may be relaxed based on the size and/or quality of POPS installed.

Sixth, the public sector should ensure that POPS are actively used by the public. Regular surveys may be carried out on POPS and/or within the neighbourhood to see whether POPS function effectively as public space. The policy regarding the use of POPS in Teheran-ro is a good strategy to promote the use of POPS. It is important, however, to lower the threshold for application and remove unnecessary complexity from the process.

Seventh, apart from the public and private sectors, more engagement of the public in POPS is desirable. The public and public authority participation used in Mediaspree area is a good instrument since it allows people other than local planning officers and building owners to express their ideas and opinions. To promote higher public participation, it is important to increase the knowledge of the public about POPS. Also, various channels should be developed to approach diverse groups of people. A well-maintained database, for example, would allow the public to not only inform themselves, but also to actively engage by sharing comments, photos and making complaints. Such a database should be monitored by city planners; when complaints are submitted, they should carry out the relevant inspections. In addition, a civic organisation could possibly be engaged to link all the relevant actors and promote their engagement with POPS, thereby encouraging wider use of POPS.

8.4.3.   Final words and implications for future research

The aim of this research was to make the following contributions to the literature: (a) to inform urban planners and policymakers about the possible challenges they may face in providing and managing public space in rapidly changing situations; (b) to suggest how the planning practice to provide and manage POPS can be improved; and (c) to add to the body of knowledge on POPS in Germany. Before concluding the book, a number of implications for future research should also be noted.

Although the focus of this study is solely on POPS, it also provides a certain level of insight into the planning cultures of South Korea and Germany and their similarities and differences in responding to urban transformation. As an example, the research demonstrates the division of competence and power at different levels of government in South Korea and Germany. Planning in both countries is decentralised but to a varying extent. The devolution of power is more observed in Germany. Indeed, the federal system in Germany is based on the notion that 'every decision should be made at the lowest possible political level' (Scholl et al., 2007, 17), as exemplified by the two-level government of Berlin, where the Senate and the districts both yield considerable powers, enabling each district to react quickly to changing circumstances.

Another difference is that the plan, and eventually the plan procedure (e.g., participation, negotiation) is more relevant in Germany than in South Korea. When it comes to urban transformation, a procedural approach is beneficial as it allows for flexibility and adaptation. Hence, in theory, it can handle the changing situation more effectively. On the other hand, the German approach is strongly plan-led, which hampers the positive effect of procedural planning. Moreover, as the Mediaspree case studies highlight, this approach is focused on the means of planning and not the ends, which has a definitive impact on urban spaces.

In contrast, South Korea takes a more substantive (e.g., design) and rule-following approach, which inhibits rapid responses to changing situations. The fact that districts in South Korea have less power than in Germany further diminishes the ability of planners to act quickly. Nevertheless, legislation, guidelines and standards are continuously and regularly amended, thereby remedying these shortcomings. This is possible due to the constant monitoring, which is rather missing in German case.

Lastly, a general difference is also found in engaging the public in planning process. Whereas citizen's engagement regarding POPS is rather limited in both cases, in Germany, the possibility to participate in the planning of POPS is still given. Although this research is devoted to POPS only, it can serve as a useful foundation for further research on planning culture and urban transformation.

I would also like to mention that more research is desirable on POPS, or co-produced public space in general. During my PhD, for instance, I found out that exclusion and underuse are regarded as the persistent problems of POPS in South Korea. So, I conducted further research on POPS in South Korea and published a paper in *Urban Research and Practice*. This paper considers why well-equipped and highly accessible POPS can still be exclusive or underused. Based on empirical work, the paper argues that this problem relates to the lack of knowledge and awareness of POPS as public spaces. Hence, it adds further recommendations to the existing suggestions.

During my PhD research in Germany, I often had the impression that public space here is understood as publicly owned spaces. So I examined to what extent POPS are relevant and needed in German cities, where private-sector involvement may be more limited than in countries with more liberal systems of governance. The findings challenge the commonly held perception that public spaces in Germany are solely or primarily publicly provided. It also suggests that private stakeholders are important partners in the provision of public spaces, and co-produced public spaces like POPS are already part of the urban reality in Germany. The research result is published in *Journal of Urban Design*. More academic research on POPS will be indispensable given the lack of knowledge on the subject. In general, future research should provide greater insight into how public spaces in Germany are co-produced and co-managed and why.

Glossary

Korean-English
건축법: Building Act
건축법시행령: Presidential Decree of Building Act
공공공간: Public space
공개공지: POPS
공공공지: Vacant public land
국토의계획및이용에관한법률: National Land Planning and Utilisation Act
국토의계획및이용에 관한 법률시행령: Presidential Decree of National Land Planning and Utilisation Act
도시 및 주거환경정비법: Act on the Maintenance and Improvement of Urban Areas and Dwelling Conditions for Residents
대지 내 공지: Vacant lot within building site
서울특별시건축물심의기준: Seoul Building Review Standards
서울특별시건축조례: Seoul Metropolitan Government Ordinance on Building (in short: Seoul Ordinance on Building)
서울특별시공개공지 설치가이드라인: Seoul POPS Provision Guideline
서울특별시지구단위계획수립기준: Guideline for Seoul District-Unit Planning (in short: Seoul DUP Guideline)
전면공지: Setback area
조경공간: Landscaping of building site
지구단위계획: District-unit planning
2025 서울특별시도시환경정비기본계획: 2025 Seoul Basic Plan of Maintenance and Improvement of Urban Areas (in short: Seoul Basic Plan)

German-English
Bauaufsichtsbehörde: Building supervisory authority
Baugrenze: Set-back line
Baulast: Public easement

Baulastenverzeichnis: Public easement register
Bauleitplanung: Urban land-use planning
Bauleitpläne: Urban land-use plans
Baulinie: Building line
Baunutzungsverordnung: Federal Land Utilisation Ordinance
Bauordnung für Berlin: Building Regulation of Berlin
Bebauungsplan/B-Plan: Legally binding land-use plan
Bebauungstiefe: Coverage depths
Begründung zum Bebauungsplan: Explanatory statement of legally binding land-use plan
Bereichsentwicklungsplanung: District development planning
Bundesnaturschutzgesetz: Federal Nature Conservation Act
Bürgerliches Gesetzbuch: Civil Code
Eingriffsregelung: Impact mitigation regulation
Flächennutzungsplan/FNP: Preparatory land-use plan
Gehrecht zu Gunsten der Allgemeinheit: Public right of way
gemischte Baufläche: Mixed-use area
Grundbuch: Land register
Grunddienstbarkeit: Easement
Grünfestsetzung: Green stipulation
Landesbauordnung: State Building Regulation
Landesnaturschutzgesetz: State Nature Conservation Acts
Landschaftsplanung: Landscape planning
Landschaftsprogramm: Landscape programme
nicht überbaubare Fläche: Non-coverable area
Planzeichnung: Zoning map
Planwerk: Area planning concept
Planwerk Innere Stadt: Area planning concept for city centre
Senatsverwaltung für Stadtentwicklung und Wohnen: Senate Department for Urban Development and Housing
städtebaulicher Vertrag: Urban development contract
textliche Darstellung: Written policies
Städtebaurecht: Urban Planning Legislation
überbaubare Fläche: Coverable area
Wasserlagenentwicklungsplan/WEP: Waterfront development plan of Berlin

Appendix

Appendix A: List of documents for document analysis

Chapter 4 (Part I)

Title	Author/Year
강남개발계획	강명구/Kang (2015)
강남의 도시공간형성과 1960년대 도시계획 상황에 대한 연구	강부성외/Kang et al. (1999)
도시계획의 변천	서울특별시/City of Seoul (n.d.)
서울 20세기 공간변천사	김광중외/Kim et al. (2001)
서울시 도시환경정비사업내공개공지 활성화를 위한 제도개선에 관한 연구	김도경외/Kim et al. (2011)
테헤란로 도시개발과정의 특성과 도시계획적 함의	허윤주/Heo (2011)
테헤란로변 공개공지의 이용실태 분석에 관한 연구	강윤희외/Kang et al. (2009)
한국 공동주택계획의 역사	윤은정외/Youn et al. (2009)
Blessing or curse? Appreciation, amenities and resistance around the Berlin 'Media-spree'	Gabriel M. Ahlfeldt (2010)
Land value	The Seoul Research Data Service (n.d.)
Mediaspree: Berlins disputed location by the water	Aljoscha Hofmann (2018)
Seoul, South Korea Population	PopulationStat (2020)

Source: Author's own table.

Chapter 4 (Part II)

Title	Author/Year
Spree riverbank for everyone! What remains of "Sink Mediaspree"?	Jan Dohnke (2014)
Vorlage zur Kenntnisnahme – Bürger-entscheid "Spreeufer für alle"	Bezirksamt FHKR von Berlin (2009a)

Source: Author's own table.

Chapter 5 (Part I)

Title	Author/Year
건축법 (시행 2019.2.15.), 법률 제15721호, 2018.8.14., 일부개정	국가법령정보센터/ Korea Law Information Center (2019)
건축법 시행령 (시행 2018.10.18.), 대통령령 제 29235호, 2018.10.16., 일부개정	국가법령정보센터/ Korea Law Information Center (2018b)
공개공지 사용 세부기준 고시 (서울특별시고시 제2017-72호)	서울특별시/ City of Seoul (2017)
국토의 계획 및 이용에 관한 법률 (시행 2018. 9.13), 법률제15671호, 2018.6.12.,일부개정	국가법령정보센터/ Korea Law Information Center (2018a)
국토의 계획 및 이용에 관한 법률 시행령 (시행 2018.11.13.), 대통령령 제29284호, 2018.11.13., 일부개정	국가법령정보센터/ Korea Law Information Center (2018c)
도심 지구단위계획구역 공개공지제도 개선 방안	박현찬외/ Park et al (2016)
서울특별시 건축 조례 (시행 2018.10.4.), 조례 제 6916호 ,1018.10.4.,타법개정	국가법령정보센터/ Korea Law Information Center (2018d)
서울특별시 건축물 심의기준 (서울특별시 공고 제2018-2012호)	서울특별시/ City of Seoul (2018)
서울특별시 공개공지 설치 가이드라인(2015)	서울특별시/ City of Seoul (2015)

Source: Author's own table.

Chapter 5 (Part II)

Title	Author/Year
서울특별시 지구단위계획 수립기준 (2016.12.)	서울특별시 / City of Seoul (2016b)
2025년 목표 서울특별시 도시,주거환경정 비기본계획(도시환경정비사업부문)	서울특별시 / City of Seoul (2016a)

Source: Author's own table.

Chapter 6 (Part I)

Title	Author/Year
About Interreg	Interreg (n.d.)
Ausführungsvorschriften zu § 4 Abs. 2 des Gesetzes zur Ausführung des Baugesetzbuches (AGBauGB)	Senatsverwaltung für Stadtentwicklung/SenStadt (2011)
Availability of Public, Near-residential Green Spaces 2016	Senatsverwaltung für Stadtentwicklung und Wohnen/SenSW (2017)
Baugesetzbuch (BauGB)	Bundesministerium der Justiz und für Verbraucherschutz/BMJV (n.d.-a)
Baugesetzbuch Kommentar	Ulrich Battis et al. (2016)
Baugesetzbuch Kommentar	Werner Ernst et al. (2018)
Baugesetzbuch Kommentar	Willy Spannowsky et al. (2018)
Baugesetzbuch mit BauGB-MaßnG Kommentar	Günter Gaentzsch (1991)
Bauordnung für Berlin (BauO Bln)	Berliner Vorschrifteninformationssystem (n.d.)
Bau- und Planungsrecht	Klaus Rabe et al. (2014)
Begründung zum Bebauungsplan V-3	Bezirksamt FHKR von Berlin (2004d)
Begründung zum Bebauungsplan V-74	Bezirksamt FHKR von Berlin (2005c)

Source: Author's own table.

Chapter 6 (Part II)

Title	Author/Year
Bereichsentwicklungsplanung FHKR Nutzungskonzept	Bezirksamt FHKR von Berlin (2005d)
Bereichsentwicklungsplanung für den Bezirk Friedrichshain-Kreuzberg (BEP 2005)	Bezirksamt FHKR von Berlin (2007a)
Berlin Environmental Atlas. Availability of Public, Near-Residential Green Spaces (Edition 2017)	Senatsverwaltung für Stadtentwicklung und Wohnen/SenSW (n.d.-a)
Berlin Kreuzberg-Spreeufer	Städtebauförderung (n.d.)
Berlin Strategy. Urban Development Concept Berlin 2030 (2015)	Senatsverwaltung für Stadtentwicklung und Wohnen/SenSW (2015a)
Berliner Modell der kooperativen Baulandentwicklung	Senatsverwaltung für Stadtentwicklung und Wohnen/SenSW (2018)
Bürgerliches Gesetzbuch (BGB)	Bundesministerium der Justiz und für Verbraucherschutz/BMJV (n.d.-b)
Das Planungslabor und seine Studierende gewinnen beim "Ideenaufruf Kreuzberger Ufer"	Marcus Jeutner (2011)
Die Innere Stadtspree. Zwischen Treptower Park und Charlottenburger Schlossbrücke. Gestaltungsleitlinien	Senatsverwaltung für Stadtentwicklung/SenStadt (2001a)
Eingeladener landschaftsplanerischer Realisierungswettbewerb. Spreeufer/Arena am Ostbahnhof (2003)	Senatsverwaltung für Stadtentwicklung/SenStadt (2003)
Entscheidungen des Bundesverfassungsgerichts	Bundesverfassungsgericht (n.d.)
Entwicklung der Berliner Wasserlagen Vorgestellt. Pressmitteilung vom 04.12.2002	Der Regierende Bürgermeister Senatskanzlei (2002)

Source: Author's own table.

Chapter 6 (Part III)

Title	Author/Year
Environmental Atlas	Senatsverwaltung für Stadtentwicklung und Wohnen/SenSW (n.d.-b)
Example of urban development contract regarding green space in Mediaspree area (Model contract)	Bezirksamt FHKR von Berlin (n.d.)
Flächennutzungsplan Berlin, Neubekanntmachung 2015	Senatsverwaltung für Stadtentwicklung und Wohnen/SenSW (2015a)
Forum Stadtspree	Planergemeinschaft (2013)
Gesetz über Naturschutz und Landschaftspflege (BNatSchG)	Bundesministerium der Justiz und für Verbraucherschutz/BMJV (n.d.-c)
Ideenaufruf Kreuzberger Ufer	Initiativkreis Mediaspre Versenken! AG Spreeufer (2010)
Ideenaufruf Kreuzberger Ufer. Modellprojekt direkter Bürgerbeteiligung an Stadtplanung. Ergebnisse der 11 Monate des offenen Ideenaufruf	Initiativkreis Mediaspre Versenken! AG Spreeufer (2012)
Kapitel 1210 – Stadt- und Freiraumplanung – Titel 526 08 – Untersuchung für räumliche Entwicklungsplanung und übergeordnete Entwicklungsvorhaben	Senatsverwaltung für Stadtentwicklung/ SenStadt (2002)
Kommunale Planung. Wasserlagenentwicklungsplan Berlin	Senatsverwaltung für Stadtentwicklung/ SenStadt (2005)
Land use planning Berlin	Senatsverwaltung für Stadtentwicklung und Wohnen/SenSW (n.d.-c)
Land use planning Berlin. Explanatory comments on the land use plan and the involvement of the public strategic planning objectives	Senatsverwaltung für Stadtentwicklung und Wohnen/SenSW (n.d.-d)
Land use planning Berlin. Land use plan – written policies	Senatsverwaltung für Stadtentwicklung und Wohnen/SenSW (n.d.-e)

Source: Author's own table.

Chapter 6 (Part IV)

Title	Author/Year
Land use planning Berlin. Relationship between land use plan and landscape programme (LaPro)	Senatsverwaltung für Stadtentwicklung und Wohnen/SenSW (n.d.-f)
Land use planning Berlin. Strategic basis – integration of land use planning into statewide and regional planning policies	Senatsverwaltung für Stadtentwicklung und Wohnen/SenSW (n.d.-g)
Land use planning Berlin. The land use plan as framework for local development plans	Senatsverwaltung für Stadtentwicklung und Wohnen/SenSW (n.d.-h)
Landschaftsprogramm. Artenschutzprogramm. Begründung und Erläuterung	Senatsverwaltung für Umwelt, Verkehr und Klimaschutz/SenUVK (2016a)
Landschaftsprogramm. Artenschutzprogramm (Broschüre)	Senatsverwaltung für Umwelt, Verkehr und Klimaschutz/SenUVK (2017)
Landschaftsprogramm einschließlich Artenschutzprogramm. Erholung und Freiraumnutzung. Entwicklungsziele und Maßnahmen	Senatsverwaltung für Umwelt, Verkehr und Klimaschutz/SenUVK (2016b)
LaPro Beschlussfassung: Erholung und Freiraumnutzung (Programmplan)	Senatsverwaltung für Stadtentwicklung und Wohnen/SenSW (2016)
Leitbild Spreeraum Friedrichshain-Kreuzberg	Senatsverwaltung für Stadtentwicklung und Wohnen/SenSW (n.d.-i)
Mitteilung – zur Kenntnisnahme – Entwicklung des Spreeraums	Der Senat von Berlin (2008)
Öffentliches Baurecht. Grundzüge des Bauplanungs- und Bauordnungsrechts unter Berücksichtigung des Raumordnungs- und Fachplanungsrechts	Franz-Joseph Peine (1993)
Planwerk Innere Stadt. Obere Stadtspree	Senatsverwaltung für Stadtentwicklung und Wohnen/SenSW (n.d.-j)
Spreeraum Friedrichshain-Kreuzberg. Leitbilder und Konzepte	Senatsverwaltung für Stadtentwicklung/SenStadt (2001b)

Source: Author's own table.

Chapter 6 (Part V)

Title	Author/Year
Stadtumbau West. Berlin Kreuzberg-Spreeufer. Voruntersuchung/Machbarkeitsstudie	Bezirksamt FHKR von Berlin (2007b)
Stadtumbau West Voruntersuchung – Kreuzberg – Spreeufer	Senatsverwaltung für Stadtentwicklung/SenStadt (2005)
The planning system and planning terms in Germany: A glossary	Elke Pahl-Weber et al. (2008)
Urban Development Concept Berlin 2030	Senatsverwaltung für Stadtentwicklung und Wohnen/SenSW (n.d.-k)
Urbanes Grün in der doppelten Innenentwicklung	Jutta Böhm et al. (2016)
Verordnung über die bauliche Nutzung der Grundstücke (BauNVO)	Bundesministerium der Justiz und für Verbraucherschutz/BMJV (n.d.-d)
Vorlage zur Kenntnisnahme – Planungsleitlinien für das Kreuzberger Spreeufer	Bezirksamt FHKR von Berlin (2009b)
Wohnungsneubau. Berliner Modell	Senatsverwaltung für Stadtentwicklung und Wohnen/SenSW (n.d.-l)
20 Green Walks in Berlin. Timeline	Senatsverwaltung für Umwelt, Verkehr und Klimaschutz/SenUVK (n.d.)

Source: Author's own table.

Chapter 7

Title	Author/Year
Bebauungsplan V-3	Bezirksamt FHKR von Berlin (2004b)
Bebauungsplan V-61	Bezirksamt FHKR von Berlin (2000a)
Bebauungsplan VI-146	Bezirksamt FHKR von Berlin (2005a)
Bebauungsplan 2-7	Bezirksamt FHKR von Berlin (2004a)
Begründung zum Bebauungsplan V-3	Bezirksamt FHKR von Berlin (2004d)
Begründung zum Bebauungsplan V-61	Bezirksamt FHKR von Berlin (2000b)
Begründung zum Bebauungsplan VI-146	Bezirksamt FHKR von Berlin (2005b)
Begründung zum Bebauungsplan 2-7	Bezirksamt FHKR von Berlin (2004c)

Source: Author's own table.

Appendix B: List of interviewees for expert interview

Interviewee 1: District planning officer
Interviewee 2: District planning officer
Interviewee 3: District planning officer
Interviewee 4: District planning officer
Interviewee 5: District planning officer
Interviewee 6: District planning officer
Interviewee 7: District planning officer
Interviewee 8: City planning officer
Interviewee 9: City officer in regeneration policy
Interviewee 10: Architect
Interviewee 11: Researcher in urban planning
Interviewee 12: Researcher in urban planning
Interviewee 13: Researcher in urban planning
Interviewee 14: Researcher in urban planning
Interviewee 15: Researcher in urban planning
Interviewee 16: Building manager
Interviewee 17: Activist from an NGO

Appendix C: List of POPS for site visit and analysis

POPS Case 1: Teheran-ro 302 in Seoul, South Korea
POPS Case 2: Teheran-ro 306 in Seoul, South Korea
POPS Case 3: Teheran-ro 322 in Seoul, South Korea
POPS Case 4: Teheran-ro 326 in Seoul, South Korea
POPS Case 5: Holzmarktstr. 34 in Berlin, Germany
POPS Case 6: Mercedes Benz Arena in Berlin, Germany
POPS Case 7: Köpenicker Str. 16-17 in Berlin, Germany
POPS Case 8: Pfuelstr./Köpenicker Str. in Berlin, Germany

Appendix D: List of instruments for POPS in Teheran-ro (Korean)

Direct planning instruments	Formal planning instruments at national level	건축법
		건축법 시행령
		국토의 계획 및 이용에 관한 법률
		국토의 계획 및 이용에 관한 법률 시행령
	Formal planning instruments at city level	서울특별시 건축 조례
		서울특별시 지구단위계획 수립기준
		2025 도시주거환경정비 기본계획
	Informal planning instruments at city level	서울특별시 건축물 심의기준
		서울특별시 공개공지 설치 가이드라인

Source: Author's own table.

Appendix E: List of instruments for POPS in Mediaspree area (German)

Indirect planning instruments	Formal planning instruments	Bauleitplanung · FNP · B-Plan
		Landschaftsplanung · Landschaftsprogramm
	Informal planning instruments	Wettbewerbe/ Gutachterverfahren/ Ideenaufruf · 1992 Städtebaulicher Ideenwettbewerb "Hauptbahnhof Berlin/Spreeufer"/ 1993 Städtebaulicher Rahmenplan "Hauptbahnhof/Spreeufer"/ 1994 Rahmenplan Mühlenstraße · 2000-2001 Städtebauliche Gutachterverfahren Postareal am Ostbahnhof und Ostgüterbahnhof · 2010-2011 Ideenaufruf Kreuzberger Ufer
		Stadtplanerische Konzepte/ Stadtentwicklungskonzepte · 1999 Planwerk Innenstadt/ 2001 Leitbild Spreeraum Friedrichshain-Kreuzberg · 2009 Planungsleitlinien Kreuzberger Spreeufer · Stadtentwicklungskonzept 2030
		Bereichsentwicklungsplanung
		Umweltatlas
		1995 Regelwerk "Die Innere Stadtspree"
	Financial instruments	INTERREG II C "Wasserlagenentwicklungsplan"
		Stadtumbau West "Kreuzberg-Spreeufer"
Direct planning Instruments	Formal planning instruments	Nicht überbaubare Fläche
		Grunddienstbarkeit
		Baulast
		Städtebaulicher Vertrag
		Grünfestsetzung
		Bürger- und Behördenbeteiligung

Bibliography

A

Ahlfeldt, G. (2010). *Blessing or curse? Appreciation, amenities and resistance around the Berlin 'Mediaspree'*. From Hamburg contemporary economic discussions, No. 32. http://hdl.handle.net/10419/42240

APOPS, MAS, & Kayden, J. (n.d.). *Privately owned public space in New York City.* https://apops.mas.org/about/mission/

Asbeek Brusse, W., Van Dalen, H., & Wissink, B. (2002). *Stad en land in een nieuwe geografie: Maatschappelijke veranderingen en ruimtelijke dynamiek.* The Hague: WRR - Scientific Council for Government Policy.

B

Banerjee, T. (2001). The future of public space: Beyond invented streets and reinvented places. *Journal of the American Planning Association, 67*(1), 9-24. https://doi.org/10.1080/01944360108976352

Battis U., Krautzberger, M., & Löhr, R. P. (2016). *Baugesetzbuch Kommentar. 13. Auflage.* https://beck-online.beck.de/Home

Berding, U., Havemann, A., Pegels, J., & Perethaler, B. (2010). *Stadträume in Spannungsfeldern: Plätze, Parks und Promenaden im Schnittbereich öffentlicher und privater Aktivitäten.* Detmold: Rohn Verlag.

Berliner Vorschrifteninformationssystem. (n.d.). *Bauordnung für Berlin.* https://gesetze.berlin.de/bsbe/document/jlr-BauOBE2005rahmen

Bezirksamt FHKR von Berlin. (2009a). *Vorlage zur Kenntnisnahme. Bürgerentscheid "Spreeufer für alle".*

Bezirksamt FHKR von Berlin. (2009b). *Vorlage zur Kenntnisnahme. Planungsleitlinien für das Kreuzberger Spreeufer.*

Bezirksamt FHKR von Berlin. (2007a). *Bereichsentwicklungsplanung für den Bezirk Friedrichshain-Kreuzberg (BEP 2005) Abschlussbericht.*

Bezirksamt FHKR von Berlin. (2007b). *Stadtumbau West. Berlin Kreuzberg-Spreeufer. Voruntersuchung/Machbarkeitsstudie.* Retrieved February 20, 2019, from https://www.stadtentwicklung.berlin.de/nachhaltige-erneuerung/f ileadmin/_migrated/content_uploads/1_Broschuere_Stadtumbau_West. pdf

Bezirksamt FHKR von Berlin. (2005a). *Bebauungsplan VI-146.* https://www.be rlin.de/ba-friedrichshain-kreuzberg/verwaltung/org/vermessung/b-plae ne/abzeichnungen/0206146.jpg

Bezirksamt FHKR von Berlin. (2005b). *Begründung zum Bebauungsplan VI-146.* https://www.berlin.de/ba-friedrichshain-kreuzberg/verwaltung/org/ vermessung/b-plaene/begruendungen/0206146.pdf

Bezirksamt FHKR von Berlin. (2005c). *Begründung zum Bebauungsplan V-74.* Retrieved February 25, 2019, from https://www.berlin.de/ba-friedrichsha in-kreuzberg/verwaltung/org/vermessung/b-plaene/begruendungen/02 05074.pdf

Bezirksamt FHKR von Berlin. (2005d). *Bereichsentwicklugsplanung FHKR Nutzungskonzept.*

Bezirksamt FHKR von Berlin. (2004a). *Bebauungsplan 2-7.* https://www.berli n.de/ba-friedrichshain-kreuzberg/verwaltung/org/vermessung/b-plaene /abzeichnungen/0200007.jpg

Bezirksamt FHKR von Berlin. (2004b). *Bebauungsplan V-3.* https://www.berli n.de/ba-friedrichshain-kreuzberg/verwaltung/org/vermessung/b-plaene /abzeichnungen/0205003.jpg

Bezirksamt FHKR von Berlin. (2004c). *Begründung zum Bebauungsplan 2-7.* https://www.berlin.de/ba-friedrichshain-kreuzberg/verwaltung/org/v ermessung/b-plaene/begruendungen/0200007.pdf

Bezirksamt FHKR von Berlin. (2004d). *Begründung zum Bebauungsplan V-3.* https://www.berlin.de/ba-friedrichshain-kreuzberg/verwaltung/org/v ermessung/b-plaene/begruendungen/0205003.pdf

Bezirksamt FHKR von Berlin. (2000a). *Bebauungsplan V-61.* https://www.berli n.de/ba-friedrichshain-kreuzberg/verwaltung/org/vermessung/b-plaene /abzeichnungen/0205061.jpg

Bezirksamt FHKR von Berlin. (2000b). *Begründung zum Bebauungsplan V-61.* https://www.berlin.de/ba-friedrichshain-kreuzberg/verwaltung/org/v ermessung/b-plaene/begruendungen/0205061.pdf

BMJV. (n.d.-a). *Baugesetzbuch.* https://www.gesetze-im-internet.de/bbaug/

BMJV. (n.d.-b). *Bürgerliches Gesetzbuch.* https://www.gesetze-im-internet.de/ bgb/

BMJV. (n.d.-c). *Gesetz über Naturschutz und Landschaftspflege.* https://www.gese tze-im-internet.de/bnatschg_2009/index.html

BMJV. (n.d.-d). *Verordnung über die bauliche Nutzung der Grundstücke.* https://w ww.gesetze-im-internet.de/baunvo/

Böhm, J., Böhme, C., Bunzel, A., Kühnau, C., Landua, D., & Reinke, M. (2016). *Urbanes Grün in der doppelten Innenentwicklung.* Retrieved February 14, 2019, from https://www.bfn.de/fileadmin/BfN/service/Dokumente/sk ripten/Skript444.pdf

Booth, P. (2011). Culture, planning and path dependence. *Town Planning Review, 82*(1), 13-28. http://dx.doi.org/10.2307/27975977

Bowen, G. (2009). Document analysis as a qualitative research method. *Qualitative Research Journal, 9*(2), 27-40. https://doi.org/10.3316/QRJ0902027

Brunt, L. (1996). *Stad.* Amsterdam: Boom.

Bundesverfassungsgericht. (n.d.). *Suche nach Entscheidungen.* https://www.bu ndesverfassungsgericht.de/SiteGlobals/Forms/Suche/Entscheidungensu che_Formular.html;jsessionid=3A919CFD61E66DDD091F871B8CB85943.1 _cid377?language_=de

C

Carmona, M. (2019). Principles for public space design, planning to do better. *Urban Design International, 24,* 47-59. https://doi.org/10.1057/s41289-018-0 070-3

Carmona, M., Hanssen, G., Lamm, B., Nylund, K., Saglie, I., & Tietjen, A. (2019). Public space in an age of austerity. *Urban Design International, 24,* 241-259. https://doi.org/10.1057/s41289-019-00082-w

Carmona, M. (2010). Contemporary public space, part two: Classification. *Journal of Urban Design, 15*(2), 157-173. https://doi.org/10.1080/1357480100 3638111

Carmona, M., Tiesdell, S., Heath, T., & Oc, T. (2010). *Public places - urban spaces: The dimensions of urban design.* London: Architectural Press.

Carmona, M., De Magalhães, C., & Hammond, L. (2008), *Public space. The management dimension.* Oxon: Routledge.

Carr, S., Francis, L., Rivlin, G., & Stone, A. (1992). *Public space.* Cambridge: Cambridge University Press.

City of Seoul. (2018). *Seoul building review standard.*

City of Seoul. (2017). *Notice of detailed criteria for the use of POPS.* https://news.s eoul.go.kr/citybuild/archives/67549

City of Seoul. (2016a). *2025 Seoul basic plan of maintenance and improvement of urban areas.*

City of Seoul. (2016b). *Guideline for Seoul district unit planning.* https://opengov .seoul.go.kr/public/9523993

City of Seoul. (2015). *Seoul POPS provision guideline.* https://news.seoul.go.kr/ snap/doc.html?fn=5636c74390a7a8.65522224.hwp&rs=/wp-content/blogs .dir/23/files/2015/11/

City of Seoul (n.d.). *Transition of urban planning.* https://urban.seoul.go.kr/vie w/html/PMNU1050200000

Couch, C., & Fraser, C. (2003). Introduction: The European context and theoretical framework. In C. Chris, C. Fraser & S. Percy, *Urban regeneration in Europe (pp. 1-16).* Oxford: Blackwell Science.

Couch, C., Fraser, C., & Percy, S. (2003). *Urban regeneration in Europe.* Oxford: Blackwell Science.

Crépin, A., Biggs, R., Polasky, S., Troell, M., & De Zeeuw, A. (2012). Regime shifts and management. *Ecological Economics, 84,* 15-22. http://dx.doi.org/ 10.1016/j.ecolecon.2012.09.003

D

De Magalhães, C. (2010). Public space and the contracting-out of publicness: A framework for analysis. *Journal of Urban Design, 15*(4), 559-574. https://d oi.org/10.1080/13574809.2010.502347

De Magalhães, C., & Carmona, M. (2009). Dimensions and models of contemporary public space management in England. *Journal of Environmental Planning and Management, 52*(1), 111-129. http://dx.doi.org/10.1080/0964056 0802504704

Der Regierende Bürgermeister Senatskanzlei. (2002). *Entwicklung der Berliner Wasserlagen Vorgestellt. Pressemitteilung vom 04.12.2002.* Retrieved July 10, 2018, from https://www.berlin.de/rbmskzl/aktuelles/pressemitteilungen /2002/pressemitteilung.45858.php

Der Senat von Berlin. (2008). *Mitteilung – zur Kenntnisnahme – Entwicklung des Spreeraums.* Retrieved July 4, 2018, from http://pardok.parlament-berlin. de/starweb/adis/citat/VT/16/DruckSachen/d16-1784.pdf

Dohnke, J. (2014). Spreeufer für Alle! - Was bleibt von "Mediaspree versenken"? In A. Holm, *Reclaim Berlin - Soziale Kämpfe in der neoliberalen Stadt.* Hamburg: Verlag Assoziation A.

E

Ellin, N. (2001). Thresholds of fear: Embracing the urban shadow. *Urban Studies, 38*(5-6), 869-883. https://doi.org/10.1080%2F00420980124399

Ellin, N. (1999). *Postmodern urbanism*, rev. edn. New York: Princeton Architectural Press.

Ernst, W., Zinkahn, W., Bielenberg, W., & Krautzberger, M. (2018). *Baugesetzbuch Kommentar.* https://beck-online.beck.de/Home

F

Faludi, A., & Hamnett, S. (1975). *The study of comparative planning.* CES conference paper no 13. London: CES.

Farthing, S. (2016). *Research design in urban planning. A student's guide.* London: Sage.

Florida, R. (2002). *The rise of the creative class: And how it's transforming work, leisure, community and everyday life.* New York: Basic Books.

Folke, C., Carpenter, S., Walker, B., Scheffer, M., Chapin, T., & Rockström, J. (2010). Resilience thinking: Integrating resilience, adaptability and transformability. *Ecology and Society, 15*(4). http://www.ecologyandsociety.org/vol15/iss4/art20/

Franck, K., & Stevens, Q. (2006). *Loose space. Possibility and diversity in urban life.* Oxon: Routledge.

Franck, K., & Paxson, L. (1989). Women and urban public space. In I. Altman, & E. Zube, *Public Places and Spaces. Human Behavior and Environment (pp. 121-146).* New York: Plenum Press.

G

Gaentzsch, G. (1991). *Baugesetzbuch - BauGB mit BauGB-MaßnG. Kommentar.* Köln: Deutscher Gemeindeverlag GmbH und Verlag W. Kohlhammer GmbH.

Gospodini, A. (2006). Portraying, classifying and understanding the emerging landscapes in the post-industrial city. *Cities, 23*(5), 311-330. https://doi.org/10.1016/j.cities.2006.06.002

Goss, J. (1996). Disquiet on the waterfront: Reflections on nostalgia and utopia in the urban archetypes of festival marketplaces. *Urban Geography, 17*(3), 221-247. https://doi.org/10.2747/0272-3638.17.3.221

Groth, J., & Corijn, E. (2005). Reclaiming urbanity: Indeterminate spaces, informal actors and urban agenda setting. *Urban Studies, 42*(3), 503-526. https://doi.org/10.1080%2F00420980500035436

H

Harvey, D. (2000). *Megacities lecture 4: Possible urban worlds*. Amersfoort, The Netherlands: Twynstra Gudde Management Consultants.

Haussermann, H. (1996). From the socialist to the capitalist city: Experiences from Germany. In G. Andrusz, M. Harloe, & I. Szelenyi (Eds.), *Cities after socialism: Urban and regional change and conflict in post-socialist societies* (pp. 214-231). Malden, MA: Blackwell.

Heo, Y. (2011). *Characteristics of development process of Teheran-ro and its implication for urban planning*. Seoul: University of Seoul.

Hillier, B. (1996). *Space is the machine: A configurational theory of architecture*. Cambridge: Cambridge University Press.

Hirt, S. (2014). *The post-public city: Experiences from post-socialist Europe. Globalizing architecture: Flows and disruptions*. Referred proceedings of the 102nd annual conference of the associations of Collegiate School of Architecture, 123-129.

Hirt, S. (2006). Post-socialist urban forms: Notes from Sofia. *Urban Geography, 27*(5), 464-488. https://doi.org/10.2747/0272-3638.27.5.464

Hofmann, A. (2018). Mediaspree: Berlin's disputed location by the water. In H. Bodenschatz, D. Frick, A. Hofmann, & X. Yi, *Europäischer Städtebau*. Beijing: China Architecture & Building Press.

I

Initiativkreis Mediaspree Versenken! AG Spreeufer. (2012). *Ideenaufruf Kreuzberger Ufer. Modellprojekt direkter Bürgerbeteiligung an Stadtplanung. Ergebnisse der 11 Monate des offenen Idennaufrufs*. Retrieved February 25, 2019, from https://issuu.com/ms-versenken/docs/austellungskatalog_webreader

Interreg. (n.d.). *About Interreg*. Retrieved July 10, 2018, from https://www.interreg.de/INTERREG2014/EN/INTERREG/AboutInterreg/aboutinterreg_node.html

Iwaniec, D., Cook, E., Barbosa, O., & Grimm, N. (2019). The framing of urban sustainability transformations. *Sustainability, 11*(573), 1-10. https://doi.org/10.3390/su11030573

J

Jenkins, P., Smith, H., & Wang, Y. (2007). *Planning and housing in the rapidly urbanising world.* Oxon: Routledge.

Jeutner, M. (2011). *Das Planungslabor und seine Studierende gewinnen beim "Ideenaufruf Kreuzberger Ufer".* Retrieved February 25, 2019, from http://ula b.architektur.tu-berlin.de/weblog/index.php?post/2011/11/03/Das-Planu nglabor-und-seine-Studierende-gewinnen-beim-Ideenaufruf-Kreuzber ger-Ufer

Jick, T. D. (1979). Mixing qualitative and quantitative methods: Triangulation in action. *Administrative science quarterly,* 24(4), 602-611. https://doi.org/10. 2307/2392366

K

Kang, B. et al. (1999). *History of the planning of Korean multi-family housing.* Se-jinsa.

Kang, M. (2015). *Gangnam development planning.* https://seoulsolution.kr/ko/n ode/3072

Kang, Y., Jung, D., & Je, H. (2009). *A study on the user's behavior analysis of public open space in Teheran-ro street.* Conference of Urban Design Institute of Korea. Urban Design Institute of Korea, 315-324.

Katz, C. (2006). Power, space and terror: Social reproduction and the public environment. In S. Low, & N. Smith, *The Politics of Public Space* (pp. 105-121). New York: Routledge.

Kayden, J., New York City Department of Planning, & Municipal Art Society. (2000). *Privately owned public space: The New York City experience.* New York: John Wiley and Sons.

Kim, D., & Kim, K. (2011). A study on the improvement of legal policies for activating public open space in urban environment improving project of Seoul city. *Journal of the Korean Institute of Lanscape Architecture,* 39(5), 21-32. https://doi.org/10.9715/KILA.2011.39.5.021

Kim, G., Son, S., Son, J., Youn, I. Youn. C., Lee, G., Lee, G., Lee, H., Choi, S., & Hwang, G. (2001). *Seoul, twentieth century: Growth & change of the last 100 years.* The Seoul Institute.

Kohn, M. (2004). *Brave new neighbourhoods: The privatisation of public space.* London: Routledge.

Korea Law Information Center. (2019). *Building Act.* https://www.law.go.kr/% EB%B2%95%EB%A0%B9/%EA%B1%B4%EC%B6%95%EB%B2%95

Korea Law Information Center. (2018a). *National land planning and utilisation act*. https://www.law.go.kr/%EB%B2%95%EB%A0%B9/%EA%B5%AD%ED%86%A0%EC%9D%98%EA%B3%84%ED%9A%8D%EB%B0%8F%EC%9D%B4%EC%9A%A9%EC%97%90%EA%B4%80%ED%95%9C%EB%B2%95%EB%A5%A0

Korea Law Information Center. (2018b). *Presidential decree of building act*. https://www.law.go.kr/%EB%B2%95%EB%A0%B9/%EA%B1%B4%EC%B6%95%EB%B2%95%EC%8B%9C%ED%96%89%EB%A0%B9

Korea Law Information Center. (2018c). *Presidential decree of national land planning and utilis/ation act*. https://www.law.go.kr/%EB%B2%95%EB%A0%B9/%EA%B5%AD%ED%86%A0%EC%9D%98%EA%B3%84%ED%9A%8D%EB%B0%8F%EC%9D%B4%EC%9A%A9%EC%97%90%EA%B4%80%ED%95%9C%EB%B2%95%EB%A5%A0%EC%8B%9C%ED%96%89%EB%A0%B9

Korea Law Information Center. (2018d). *Seoul metropolitan government ordinance on building*. https://www.law.go.kr/%EC%9E%90%EC%B9%98%EB%B2%95%EA%B7%9C/%EC%84%9C%EC%9A%B8%ED%8A%B9%EB%B3%84%EC%8B%9C%EA%B1%B4%EC%B6%95%EC%A1%B0%EB%A1%80

Kovács, Z. (1999). Cities from state-socialism to global capitalism: An introduction. *GeoJournal, 49*, 1-6. http://dx.doi.org/10.1023/A:1007048819606

Krehl, A., & Weck, S. (2020). Doing comparative case study research in urban and regional studies: What can be learnt from practice? *European Planning Studies, 9*, 1858-1876. https://doi.org/10.1080/09654313.2019.1699909

L

Langstraat, F., & Van Melik, R. (2013). Challenging the 'end of public space': A comparative analysis of publicness in Britisch and Dutch urban spaces. *Journal of Urban Design, 18*(3), 429-448. https://doi.org/10.1080/13574809.2013.800451

Lee, D. (2020). Whose space is privately owned public space? Exclusion, underuse and the lack of knowledge and awareness. *Urban Research & Practice*. https://doi.org/10.1080/17535069.2020.1815828

Lee, D., & Scholten, N. (2022). Do welfare states need privately owned public spaces? The relevance of and need for such spaces in German cities. *Journal of Urban Design*. https://doi.org/10.1080/13574809.2022.2036110

Lefebvre, H. (1990). *The production of space*. Oxford: Blackwell.

Lofland, L. (1998). *The public realm: Exploring the city's quintessential social territory*. New York: Aldine de Gruyter.

Loukaitou-Sideris, A. (1993). Privatisation of public open space: The Los Angeles experience. *The Town Planning Review, 62*(2), 139-167. https://doi.org/1 0.3828/tpr.64.2.6h26535771454436

Loukaitou-Sideris, A., & Banerjee, T. (1998). *Urban design downtown: Poetics and politics of form.* Berkeley: University of Califonia Press.

M

Madanipour, A. (2003). *Public and private spaces of the city.* London: Routledge.

Miao, P. (2001). Introduction. In P. Miao (Ed.), *Public Places in Asia Pacific Cities (pp. 1-45).* Dordrecht: Kluwer Academic Publishers.

Minton, A. (2006). *What kind of world are we building? The privatisation of public space.* London: RICS.

N

Németh, J., & Schmidt, S. (2011). The privatisation of public space: Modeling and measuring publicness. *Environment and Planning B: Planning and Design, 38*(1), 5-23. https://doi.org/10.1068%2Fb36057

Neugebauer, C., & Rekhviashvili, L. (2015). Loss and (re-)construction of public space in post-Soviet cities. *International Journal of Sociology and Social Policy, 35*(7/8). https://doi.org/10.1108/IJSSP-04-2015-0042

Nissen, S. (2008). Urban transformation. From public and private space to spaces of hybrid character. *Czech Sociological Review, 44*(6), 1129-1149. http:/ /dx.doi.org/10.13060/00380288.2008.44.6.04

Nuissl, H., & Rink, D. (2005). The 'production' of urban sprawl in eastern Germany as a phenomenon of post-socialist transformation. *Cities, 22*(2), 123-134. https://doi.org/10.1016/j.cities.2005.01.002

O

Oldenburg, R. (1989). *The great good place: Cafés, coffee shops, community centers, beauty parlors, general stores, bars, hangouts, and how they get you through the day.* New York: Paragon House.

Orum, A., & Neal, Z. (2009). *Common ground? Readings and reflections on public space.* NY: Routledge.

P

Pahl-Weber, E., & Henckel, D. (2008). *The planning system and planning terms in Germany: A glossary.* Hanover: Akademie für Raumforschung und Landesplanung (ARL).

Park, H., & Yang, E. (2016). *Improvement of the Privately Owned Public Space in the district planning area.* Seoul: The Seoul Institute.

Patton, M. (1990). *Qualitative evaluation and research methods (2nd ed.).* Newbury Park, CA: Sage.

Peine, F.-J. (1993). *Öffentliches Baurecht: Grundzüge des Bauplanungs- und Bauordnungsrechts unter Berücksichtigung des Raumordnungs- und Fachplanungsrechts.* Tübingen: J. C. B. Mohr (Paul Siebeck).

Planergemeinschaft. (2013). *Forum StadtSpree. Reader zur Vorbereitung auf die erste Veranstaltung am 30.1.2013 im Radialsystem V.* https://www.stadtspree.org/wp-content/uploads/2013/01/FSt_2013-01-28_Reader_web.pdf

PopulationStat. (2020). *Seoul, South Korea population.* Retrieved July 22, 2020, from PopulationStat. World statistical data: https://populationstat.com/south-korea/seoul#:~:text=The%20most%20densely%20populated%20in%20othe%20world&text=There%20are%2017%2C000%20people%20per,packed%20into%20600%2Dsquare%20kilometers.

Punter, J. (1990). The privatisation of the public realm. *Planning Practice & Research, 5*(3), 8-16. https://doi.org/10.1080/02697459008722771

R

Rabe, K., Pauli, F., & Wenzel, G. (2014). *Bau- und Planungsrecht.* Stuttgart: Deutscher Gemeindeverlag GmbH u. Verlag W. Kohlhammer GmbH.

Ritchie, H., & Roser, M. (2018). *Our world in data.* Retrieved August 12, 2020, from Urbanization: https://ourworldindata.org/urbanization

Rubin, M. (2020). *Densifying the city? Global cases and Johannesburg.* Northampton, Massachusetts: Edward Elgar Publishing.

S

Scholl, B., Elgendy, H., & Nollert, M. (2007). *Raumplanung in Deutschland - formeller Aufbau und zukünftige Aufgaben.* Karlsruhe: Universitätsverlag Karlsruhe.

SenStadt. (2016). *Landschaftsprogramm einschließlich Artenschutzprogramm.* Retrieved July 5, 2018, from Landschaftsprogramm, Artenschutzprogramm.

Begründung und Erläuterung 2016: https://www.berlin.de/senuvk/umwe
lt/landschaftsplanung/lapro/download/lapro_begruendung_2016.pdf

SenStadt. (2011). *Ausführungsvorschriften zu § 4 Abs. 2 des Gesetzes zur Ausführung des Baugesetzbuches (AGBauGB)*. Retrieved February 26, 2019,
from https://stadtentwicklung.berlin.de/service/gesetzestexte/de/downl
oad/AV_BEP.pdf

SenStadt. (2005a). *Kommunale Planung. Wasserlagenentwicklungsplan Berlin*. Retrieved February 20, 2019, from https://docplayer.org/57594297-Wasserla
genentwicklungsplan-berlin.html

SenStadt. (2005b). *Stadtumbau West Voruntersuchung - Kreuzberg - Spreeufer*.
Retrieved February 20, 2019, from https://www.stadtentwicklung.berlin.
de/nachhaltige-erneuerung/fileadmin/_migrated/content_uploads/Voru
ntersuchung_Kreuzberg-Spreeufer_Dezember_2005_01.pdf

SenStadt. (2003). *Eingeladener landschaftsplanerischer Realisierungswettbewerb.
Spreeufer/Arena am Ostbahnhof*. Retrieved February 21, 2019, from https:/
/www.competitionline.com/upload/downloads/xx/2_Auslobung.pdf

SenStadt. (2002). *Kapitel 1210 - Stadt- und Freiraumplanung - Titel 526 08 - Un-
tersuchung für räumliche Entwicklungsplanung und übergeordnete Entwick-
lungsvorhaben*. Retrieved February 20, 2019, from https://www.parlamen
t-berlin.de/ados/Haupt/vorgang/h15-0222-v.pdf

SenStadt. (2001a). *Die Innere Stadtspree. Zwischen Treptower Park und Charlottenburger Schlossbrücke. Gestaltungsleitlinien*.

SenStadt. (2001b). *Spreeraum Friedrichshain-Kreuzberg. Leitbilder und Konzepte*.
Retrieved February 21, 2019, from https://www.stadtentwicklung.berlin.
de/planen/stadtplanerische_konzepte/leitbild_spreeraum/download/bro
schuere_spreeraum.pdf

SenSW. (2018). *Berliner Modell der kooperativen Baulandentwicklung*. Retrieved
February 1, 2019, from https://www.stadtentwicklung.berlin.de/wohnen
/wohnungsbau/download/vertraege/modell_baulandentwicklung.pdf

SenSW. (2017). *Availability of public, near-residential green spaces 2016*. https://fbi
nter.stadt-berlin.de/fb/index.jsp?loginkey=showMap&mapId=ek06_05g
ruenversorg2016@esenstadt&Szenario=fb_en

SenSW. (2016). *LaPro Beschlussfassung. Erholung und Freiraumnutzung (Pro-
grammplan)*. https://fbinter.stadt-berlin.de/fb/index.jsp

SenSW. (2015a). *Berlin strategy. Urban development concept Berlin 2030*. Retrieved
July 5, 2018, from https://www.stadtentwicklung.berlin.de/planen/stadte
ntwicklungskonzept/download/strategie/BerlinStrategie_Broschuere_en
.pdf

SenSW. (2015b). *Flächennutzungsplan Berlin. Neubekanntmachung Januar 2015*. Retrieved July 3, 2018, from https://www.stadtentwicklung.berlin.de/pla nen/fnp/pix/fnp/fnp_nbk_2015.pdf

SenSW. (2015c). FNP (Berlin zoning map). https://fbinter.stadt-berlin.de/fb/i ndex.jsp?Szenario=fb_en

SenSW. (n.d.-a). *Berlin environmental atlas. Availability of public, near-residential green spaces (Edition 2017)*. Retrieved July 9, 2018, from https://www.stadte ntwicklung.berlin.de/umwelt/umweltatlas/edb605_01.htm

SenSW. (n.d.-b). *Environmental Atlas*. Retrieved July 9, 2018, from https://ww w.stadtentwicklung.berlin.de/umwelt/umweltatlas/edua_index.shtml

SenSW. (n.d.-c). *Land use planning Berlin*. Retrieved July 3, 2018, from https:// www.stadtentwicklung.berlin.de/planen/fnp/index_en.shtml

SenSW. (n.d.-d). *Land Use Planning Berlin. Explanatory comments on the land use plan and the involvement of the public strategic planning objectives*. Retrieved July 3, 2018, from https://www.stadtentwicklung.berlin.de/planen/fnp/e n/fnp/strategische_ziele.shtml

SenSW. (n.d.-e). *Land use planning Berlin. Land use plan - written policies*. Re- trieved July 3, 2018, from https://www.stadtentwicklung.berlin.de/plane n/fnp/en/fnp/textliche_darstellung.shtml

SenSW. (n.d.-f). *Land use planning Berlin. Relationship between land use plan and landscape programme (LaPro)*. Retrieved July 4, 2018, from https://www.sta dtentwicklung.berlin.de/planen/fnp/en/fnp/verhaeltnis_lapro.shtml

SenSW. (n.d.-g). *Land use planning Berlin. Strategic basis - integration of land use planning into state-wide and regional planning policies*. Retrieved February 13, 2019, from https://www.stadtentwicklung.berlin.de/planen/fnp/en/strate gische_grundlagen/index.shtml

SenSW. (n.d.-h). *Land use planning Berlin. The land use plan as framework for local development plans*. Retrieved July 3, 2018, from https://www.stadtentwickl ung.berlin.de/planen/fnp/en/fnp/grundsaetze_bebauungsplaenen.shtml

SenSW. (n.d.-i). *Leitbild Spreeraum Friedrichshain-Kreuzberg*. Retrieved July 10, 2018, from https://www.stadtentwicklung.berlin.de/planen/stadtplaneris che_konzepte/leitbild_spreeraum/

SenSW. (n.d.-j). *Planwerk Innere Stadt. Obere Stadtspree*. Retrieved July 10, 2018, from https://www.stadtentwicklung.berlin.de/planen/planwerke/de/pla nwerk_innere_stadt/raeumliche_schwerpunkte/obere_stadtspree/index. shtml

SenSW. (n.d.-k). *Urban dvelopment concept Berlin 2030.* Retrieved February 23, 2019, from https://www.stadtentwicklung.berlin.de/planen/stadtentwick lungskonzept/index_en.shtml

SenSW. (n.d.-l). *Wohnungsneubau. Berliner Modell.* Retrieved February 1, 2019, from https://www.stadtentwicklung.berlin.de/wohnen/wohnungsbau/de /vertraege/index.shtml

SenUVK. (2017). *Landschaftsprogramm, Artenschutzprogramm.* Retrieved July 5, 2018, from https://www.berlin.de/senuvk/umwelt/landschaftsplanung/la pro/download/lapro_broschuere_dez_2017_text.pdf

SenUVK. (2016a). *Landschaftsprogramm. Artenschutzprogramm. Begründung und Erläuterung 2016.*

SenUVK. (2016b). *Landschaftsprogramm einschließlich Artenschutzprogramm. Erholung und Freiraumnutzung. Entwicklungsziele und Maßnahmen.* Retrieved July 5, 2018, from https://www.berlin.de/senuvk/umwelt/landschaftsplan ung/lapro/download/lapro_broschuere_dez_2017_plan4.pdf

SenUVK. (n.d.). *20 Green walks in Berlin. Timeline.* Retrieved July 9, 2018, from https://www.berlin.de/sen/uvk/en/nature-and-green/landscape-pl anning/20-green-walks-in-berlin/timeline/

Short, J., & Kim, Y. (1999). *Globalization and the city.* Harlow: Longman.

Smithsimon, G. (2008). Dispersing the crowd: Bonus plazas and the creation of public space. *Urban Affairs Review, 43*(3), 325-351. https://doi.org/10.1177 %2F1078087407306325

Sorkin, M. (1992). *Variations on a theme park: The new American city and the end of public space.* New York: Hill and Wang.

Spannowsky, W., & Uechtritz, M. (2018). *BauGB Kommentar.* 52. Edition. Beck'sche Online-Kommentare.

Städtebauförderung. (n.d.). *Berlin Kreuzberg-Spreeufer.* Retrieved February 20, 2019, from https://www.staedtebaufoerderung.info/StBauF/DE/Progra mm/Stadtumbau/StadtumbauWest/Praxis/Kommunale_Praxisbeispiele/ Massnahmen/berlin_kreuzberg_spreeufer/berlin_kreuzbg_node.html

Stanilov, K. (2007). Democracy, markets, and public space in the transitional societies of Central and Eastern Europe. In K. Stanilov (Ed.), *The Post-Socialist City: Urban Form and Space Transformations in Central and Eastern Europe after Socialism (pp. 269-283).* Dordrecht: Springer.

Stevens, Q. (2007). *The ludic city. Exploring the potential of public spaces.* Oxon: Routledge.

Stolk, S. (2013). New York groener door privaat initiatief. *Agora, 29,* 12-15. htt ps://doi.org/10.21825/agora.v29i2.2028

T

The Seoul Research Data Service. (n.d.). *Land value.* http://data.si.re.kr/node/
    93
Tilly, C. (1984). *Big structures, large processes, huge comparisons.* Russel Sage Foun-
    dation.

U

United Nations. (2018). *World urbanization prospects 2018. Percentage of population
    at mid-year residing in urban areas by region, subregion and country, 1950-2050.*
    Retrieved August 12, 2020, from https://population.un.org/wup/Downloa
    d/

V

Van Melik, R. (2008). *Changing public space. The recent development of Dutch city
    squares.* Utrecht: KNAG/Faculteit Geowetenschapen Universiteit Utrecht.
Van Melik, R., & Van der Krabben, E. (2016). Co-production of public space:
    Policy translations from New York City to the Netherlands. *The Town Plan-
    ning Review,* 87(2), 139-158. http://dx.doi.org/10.3828/tpr.2016.12
Van Melik, R., Van Aalst, I., & Van Weesep, J. (2007). Fear and fantasy in the
    public domain: The development of secured and themed urban space. *Jour-
    nal of Urban Design,* 12(1), 25-42. https://doi.org/10.1080/1357480060107117
    0
Varna, G. (2014). *Measuring public space: The star model.* Surrey: Ashgate Pub-
    lishing.
Varna, G., & Tiesdell, S. (2010). Assessing the publicness of public space: The
    star model of publicness. *Journal of Urban Design,* 15(4), 575-598. https://do
    i.org/10.1080/13574809.2010.502350
VROM. (2001). *Ruimte maken, ruimte delen: Vijfde Nota over de Ruimtelijke Orden-
    ing 2000-2020.* The Hague: Ministry of Housing, Spatial Planning and the
    Environment (VROM).

W

Webster, C. (2007). Property rights, public space and urban design. *The Town
    Planning Review,* 78(1), 81-101. http://dx.doi.org/10.3828/tpr.78.1.6
White, E. T. (1983). Site analysis: Diagramming information for architectural
    design, *Architectural Media Ltd.*

Whyte, W. (1988). *City: Rediscovering the center.* New York: Doubleday.

Wießer, R. (1999). Urban development in East Germay - Specific features of urban transformation processes. *GeoJournal, 49,* 43-51. https://doi.org/10.1 023/A:1007016912703

World Bank Group. (2015). *World Bank.* Retrieved August 12, 2020, from East Asia's changing urban landscape: Measuring a decade of spatial growth. From https://www.worldbank.org/content/dam/Worldbank/Publications /Urban%20Development/EAP_Urban_Expansion_full_report_web.pdf

Worpole, K., & Knox, K. (2007). *The social value of public spaces.* York: Joseph Rewntree Foundation.

Y

Youn, E., & Jung, I. (2009). A study on the formation of urban space in Gang-nam area and the urban discourse in the 1960s. *Journal of the Architectural Institute of Korea, 25*(5), 231-238.

Z

Zukin, S. (1998). Urban lifestyles: Diversity and standardisation in spaces of consumption. *Urban Studies, 35*(5-6), 825-839. https://doi.org/10.1080%2F 0042098984574

Social Sciences

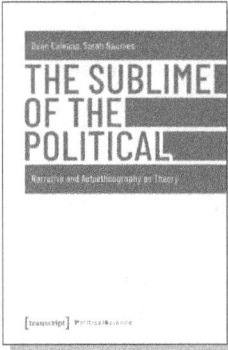

Dean Caivano, Sarah Naumes
The Sublime of the Political
Narrative and Autoethnography as Theory

July 2021, 162 p., hardcover
100,00 € (DE), 978-3-8376-4772-3
E-Book:
PDF: 99,99 € (DE), ISBN 978-3-8394-4772-7

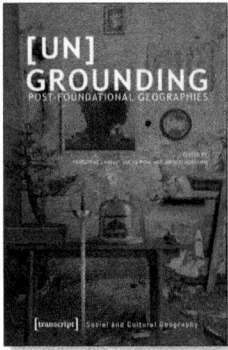

Friederike Landau, Lucas Pohl, Nikolai Roskamm (eds.)
[Un]Grounding
Post-Foundational Geographies

May 2021, 348 p., pb., col. ill.
50,00 € (DE), 978-3-8376-5073-0
E-Book:
PDF: 49,99 € (DE), ISBN 978-3-8394-5073-4

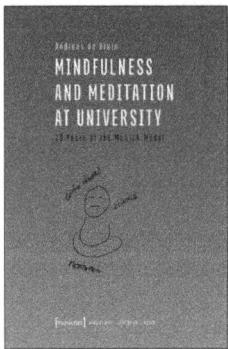

Andreas de Bruin
Mindfulness and Meditation at University
10 Years of the Munich Model

April 2021, 216 p., pb.
25,00 € (DE), 978-3-8376-5696-1
E-Book: available as free open access publication
PDF: ISBN 978-3-8394-5696-5

**All print, e-book and open access versions of the titles in our list
are available in our online shop www.transcript-publishing.com**

Social Sciences

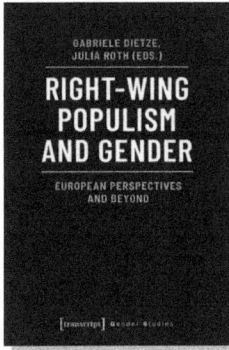

Gabriele Dietze, Julia Roth (eds.)
Right-Wing Populism and Gender
European Perspectives and Beyond

2020, 286 p., pb., ill.
35,00 € (DE), 978-3-8376-4980-2
E-Book:
PDF: 34,99 € (DE), ISBN 978-3-8394-4980-6

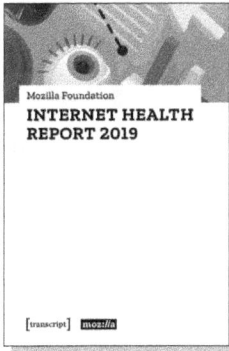

Mozilla Foundation
Internet Health Report 2019

2019, 118 p., pb., ill.
19,99 € (DE), 978-3-8376-4946-8
E-Book: available as free open access publication
PDF: ISBN 978-3-8394-4946-2

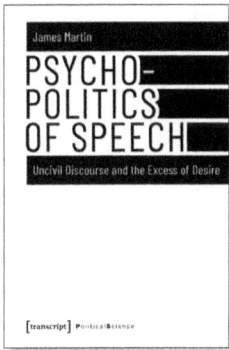

James Martin
Psychopolitics of Speech
Uncivil Discourse and the Excess of Desire

2019, 186 p., hardcover
79,99 € (DE), 978-3-8376-3919-3
E-Book:
PDF: 79,99 € (DE), ISBN 978-3-8394-3919-7

**All print, e-book and open access versions of the titles in our list
are available in our online shop www.transcript-publishing.com**

GPSR Authorized Representative: Easy Access System Europe, Mustamäe tee
50, 10621 Tallinn, Estonia, gpsr.requests@easproject.com